High-Involvement Management

*Participative Strategies
for Improving
Organizational Performance*

Edward E. Lawler III

High-Involvement Management

 Jossey-Bass Publishers

San Francisco • London • 1988

HIGH-INVOLVEMENT MANAGEMENT
Participative Strategies for Improving Organizational Performance
by Edward E. Lawler III

Copyright © 1986 by: Jossey-Bass Inc., Publishers
350 Sansome Street
San Francisco, California 94104
&
Jossey-Bass Limited
28 Banner Street
London EC1Y 8QE

Library of Congress Cataloging-in-Publication Data

Lawler, Edward E.
High-involvement management.

(The Jossey-Bass management series)
(The Jossey-Bass social and behavioral science
series)
Bibliography: p. 235
Includes index.
1. Management—Employee participation. 2. Quality
of work life. I. Title. II. Series. III. Series:
Jossey-Bass social and behavioral science series.
HD5650.L35   1986   658.3'152   85-45909
ISBN 0-87589-686-3 (alk. paper)

Manufactured in the United States of America

The paper in this book meets the guidelines for
permanence and durability of the Committee on
Production Guidelines for Book Longevity of the
Council on Library Resources.

JACKET DESIGN BY WILLI BAUM

FIRST EDITION
First printing: April 1986
Second printing: December 1986
Third printing: August 1987
Fourth printing: June 1988

Code 8615

A joint publication in
The Jossey-Bass Management Series
and
The Jossey-Bass
Social and Behavioral Science Series

Consulting Editors
Organizations and Management

Warren Bennis
University of Southern California

Richard O. Mason
Southern Methodist University

Ian I. Mitroff
University of Southern California

To Patty
for her love and involvement

Preface

Participative approaches to management offer an exciting and potentially highly effective alternative to traditional management styles. *High-Involvement Management* examines the question of whether participative management approaches can, in fact, increase organizational performance. The explosive interest in such participative programs as quality circles, gainsharing, and job enrichment makes participation a timely topic.

The entire field of management is in need of research-based treatments of what works and what does not work. Too much of what is written today simply sells new programs as the solution to management's problems. *High-Involvement Management* goes much beyond this; it analyzes the major approaches to participative management and points out when they work, where they work, and how they can be implemented. In short, it details their applicability, strengths, and weaknesses.

In this book I present, for the first time, an overview of what I have learned from my work on participative management over the last twenty-five years. As both a researcher and a consultant, I have studied and assessed the effectiveness of quality circles, attitude surveys, job enrichment, work teams, quality-of-work-life programs, gainsharing, and new-design plants, and I have helped implement hundreds of participative management programs. In most cases this research has been long-term, action-related research, and the results have been published in the scientific literature; indeed, some projects have been important enough to have books written about them. Most of my conclusions are based on these results. Thus, the views presented here are not simply my opinion; they are based on decades of research by myself and others.

Although I have always emphasized the objective assessment of organizational practices in my research, I must admit to a bias. I personally prefer organizations in which people are motivated by a sense of involvement and commitment. This has led me to focus my research on developing ways of making participation an effective strategy for most organizations.

Even though I am favorably disposed toward participative management, I am not committed to any particular approach or program. I believe it is important to critically analyze all participative approaches, and I have done just this in this book. Strong ideas should not fear responsible criticism; quite the contrary, an objective evaluation can help ideas grow, develop, and be applied more effectively. If we are to maximize the effectiveness of participatively managed organizations, criticism is a necessary part of the development of new and better ways of managing participatively.

Because participative management and organizational effectiveness are such important issues, I have written this book with a broad audience in mind. Numbers and jargon are kept to a minimum, and conclusions are carefully drawn from research studies. The issues covered are not just important for managers; they are important for all who are concerned about the design of work organizations.

Union leaders, managers, students, employees—in short, anyone interested in participative management—should find that this book provides valuable insights into how participative programs work. This book should also help these individuals design and manage their own approaches to participation.

Because this book is research-based but written with a practical orientation, it can have a number of uses. Any class on participative management should find it a valuable textbook. It should also prove a valuable training aid for organizations interested in participative management.

Overview of the Contents

Chapters One, Two, and Three set the stage for later discussion of the major participative management approaches. They point out the potential advantages and disadvantages of participation as well as present some of the basic research on organizational effectiveness. Chapter Two focuses on why the time seems right for participative management. Chapter Three analyzes what is meant by participative management and presents a useful way of predicting how effective participative management approaches are likely to be.

Chapter Four examines the most popular participative management approach, quality circles. A useful starting point for participative management programs, quality circles do not offer an effective long-term approach because of their self-destructive character. Although this view of quality circles is controversial, it is supported by considerable research evidence.

Chapter Five focuses on the use of attitude surveys. These surveys can form a valuable part of any participative management approach but are not significant enough by themselves to move an organization toward effective participative management.

Chapters Six and Seven cover two approaches to involving people more in their work: teams and job enrichment. Both are seen as valuable approaches to designing work in a participative organization, yet both need to be accompanied by other organizational changes.

Quality-of-work-life approaches to union-management relations are discussed in Chapter Eight. These approaches have proven very successful at Ford, General Motors, and other large corporations. I argue that they are the right place to start encouraging participation in an organized workplace but that they are only a first step toward the kind of involvement that is possible in an organized setting.

Preface

Gainsharing is discussed in Chapter Nine. It is particularly important because it combines financial participation with participation in decision making. Nevertheless, gainsharing often elicits only low-level participation and thus fails to maximize organizational effectiveness. New design plants are discussed in Chapter Ten. These plants represent the best approach to involving people in decisions, but, in contrast to gainsharing, they do not involve people financially.

I am most excited about the new approach to management that is presented in Chapter Eleven. This promising approach goes beyond the participative management programs discussed in the previous chapters. It involves employees in the business, both financially and psychologically, and encourages them to care more, know more, do more, and be rewarded more. This combination of outcomes is exactly what is needed if participative management is to be successful in practice. In many important features this approach goes beyond general prescriptions such as "productivity through people," "management by walking around," and "get people involved"; it describes how to design, structure, and manage a high-involvement work organization, and as a kind of blueprint for implementing participative management styles, it should be particularly useful.

Chapter Twelve describes the issues involved in changing to a participatively managed organization. Although some large corporations such as Honeywell and Xerox are making important progress, it remains difficult to change traditionally managed organizations. This chapter offers some suggestions for undertaking this change and discusses what results can be expected.

Acknowledgments

I have been fortunate to be associated with a number of outstanding researchers whose work has greatly influenced my thinking and this book. I would like to mention some by name. Mason Haire, Edwin Ghiselli, and Lyman Porter were wonderful mentors during my years as a graduate student; Porter has been a valued colleague ever since. Chris Argyris and Richard Hackman influenced my work a great deal while I was at Yale University. At the University of Michigan I worked with a number of exceptional researchers who were part of the quality of work program. Stanley Seashore, Cortland Cammann, and Robert Kahn exerted a major influence on my work, as did David Nadler, Phillip Mirvis, Dennis Perkins, Veronica Nieva, Nina Gupta, R. J. Bullock, and Douglas Jenkins. Since I have been at the University of Southern California, I have been fortunate to work with Susan A. Mohrman, Allan M. Mohrman, Jr., and Gerald E. Ledford, Jr., in the Center for Effective Organizations. Finally, I owe a great debt to the many managers, union leaders, and employees who have taught me about participative management.

Los Angeles, California   Edward E. Lawler III
March 1986

Contents

The Author

Edward E. Lawler III is professor of management and organization and research professor in the Graduate School of Business Administration at the University of Southern California. He joined the university in 1978 and during 1979 founded and became the director of the university's Center for Effective Organizations.

After receiving his B.A. degree from Brown University (1960) and his Ph.D. degree from the University of California at Berkeley (1964), both in psychology, Lawler joined the faculty of Yale University. He moved to the University of Michigan in 1972 as professor of psychology and program director in the Survey Research Center at the Institute for Social Research.

Lawler is a member of many professional organizations in his field and serves on the editorial boards of five major journals. He has served as a consultant to more than one hundred organizations on employee involvement, organizational change, and compensation and is the author and coauthor of more than one hundred articles and eleven books. His most recent books include *Organizational Assessment* (1980), *Pay and Organization Development* (1981), *Managing Creation* (1983), and *Doing Research That Is Useful for Theory and Practice* (1985).

High-Involvement Management

Participative Strategies for Improving Organizational Performance

Changing Approaches to Management

Participative management is an idea whose time has come. But it is not a new idea. Indeed, for decades the management literature has been filled with arguments for better treatment of employees, more interesting work, and more democratic supervision (see, for example, Argyris, 1957; Likert, 1961; McGregor, 1960). Until recently, however, these arguments have had little impact on how managers actually behaved and on how organizations were managed. Indeed, it often seemed as if the management theorists were talking, but no one was listening. Now many managers and companies are practicing what has been advocated for decades. In some cases they have even gone beyond accepted theory and have developed innovative management practices that improve both organizational performance and the quality of work life.

Although there is no systematic research study to prove that change is occurring, evidence of change is everywhere.

- Quality circles have grown at a dramatic rate in the last few years. Hundreds of companies organize meetings in which groups of employees address problems involving productivity and quality. One recent study found that forty out of

1

fifty-two large companies undergoing change had quality circles, most of them introduced since 1980 (Gorlin and Schein, 1984). My estimate is that over two hundred thousand American workers have been in quality circles.

- According to a Motorola advertisement, their participative management program is operating for more than 95 percent of their manufacturing employees and has been "dramatically successful" (*Newsweek,* June 17, 1985).

- Many companies are experimenting with self-managing work teams and other job-enrichment approaches designed to give employees a chance to make more of the day-to-day decisions concerning their work (Hackman and Oldham, 1980).

- A management book that advocates participation, *In Search of Excellence* (Peters and Waterman, 1982), has sold over five million copies, an unprecedented sales volume for a book on management.

- Through flex-time and flexible benefit programs, more and more people are being given a chance to decide for themselves what time they will come to work and even what fringe benefits they will receive (Lawler, 1981).

- In Ford Motor Company, General Motors (GM), and hundreds of other companies union-management steering committees are meeting to facilitate cooperative problem solving between unions and management (Lawler and Ozley, 1979).

- Honeywell, Procter & Gamble, and dozens of other companies have built new-design plants that minimize the distance between workers and managers. The plants involve employees in many decisions and are structured on the basis of work teams. In some plants employees make pay, hiring, scheduling, and quality decisions. One estimate is that hundreds of these plants exist (Walton, 1985).

- In 1974 Motorola sold its Franklin Park facility to a Japanese manufacturer. At that time for every 100 sets that rolled off the line there were 150 defects. After ten years with new owners and a more participative management style, productivity has doubled and defects have been reduced to 2 per hundred.

- Honeywell, Xerox, Motorola, Ford, General Motors (GM),

and Westinghouse have all publicly committed themselves to using a more participative approach to organizing and managing people. Their change programs are even more significant than the increased use of such practices as quality circles, gainsharing, and self-managing teams because they are trying to change the entire organization, not just a few plants or a few practices.

- I have met with the presidents of a number of large U.S. corporations that are committed to participative management (an event which simply wouldn't have occurred ten years ago) and they are impressive in their ability to discuss their change programs as well as their ability to analyze different approaches to participation. When they declare it is time for a change of this magnitude, we need to take notice.

Both company-wide programs of change and such specific programs as quality circles and attitude surveys share important common elements. These different programs all move one or more of the following further down in the organization: information, knowledge, rewards, and power. This has the effect of allowing more people to participate in important decisions and activities, and because of this, these programs are often collectively referred to as participative approaches to management.

No more fundamental change could occur than that involved in moving power, knowledge, information, and rewards to lower levels. It changes the very nature of what work is and means to everyone who works in an organization. Because it profoundly affects the jobs of everyone it can impact on the effectiveness of all work organizations. It can also affect the economic well-being of everyone in the United States. If its impact is positive, we all stand to gain. But if its impact is negative, we all stand to lose. It is vital that we understand this transformation and that we do everything we can to see that it is successful.

Possible Gains

Participative management appears to offer tremendous potential gains. If, for example, it can create organizations where people at all levels think for themselves and manage their own work, then far fewer employees will be needed and those who remain will have more rewarding and satisfying jobs. This in turn could help make the higher labor costs in the United States competitive because lower-level employees would be contributing more by using both their hands and their minds. If it causes people to care more about how they do their work, it could lead to higher-quality products that are internationally competitive.

In short, if our organizations were able to effectively utilize participative management, the gains could be tremendous. We could be a more productive society in which work positively contributes to the quality of people's lives. We could again be competitive in international markets, be admired for our management skills, and be a society whose workplaces are a source of pride and power. We might also come much closer to matching the reality of how people are treated in our workplaces with our ideal of how they should be treated: with respect; dignity; democratic rights; individual rights; and the right to share in the fruits of their labor. These values have fueled our society for over two centuries but they have not provided much power for our work organizations.

In the area of participative management the message is clear: organizations and their employees need to be aware of what is available and what makes participative management programs effective. The uninformed run the very great risk of investing millions of dollars and years of effort in programs that simply cannot work. As we shall see, some major companies are currently in this unfortunate situation.

It would be nice to report that all is going well as we make this transition to more participative approaches to management. The good news is that there is a great deal of activity; the bad news is that much of it is poorly conceived, uses the wrong approaches, and is destined to fail. Unfortunately many organizations do not effectively move rewards, power, information, and knowledge to lower levels; such organizations are bound to fail in their participative management efforts.

Fortunately, knowledge is available that can prevent major mistakes from happening. A great deal of research has been done that shows when, where, and how to initiate participative management programs to ensure that these programs will work. Some organizations are already putting this information to good use, and, as a result, are gaining a competitive advantage—we can learn from them.

It is important to understand the strengths and weaknesses of the different approaches to participative management that will be reviewed in this book. Informed choice is both possible and necessary if employees are to make effective use of participative management. Managers need to understand how it will affect their work lives just as nonmanagerial employees need to understand that their work lives will change drastically if participative management becomes a reality. It places new demands on everyone, but it also offers new rewards. New skills are needed as old skills are made obsolete; thus employees need to understand what preparation they need for participative management.

The way we presently manage most work organizations has served us well in many respects. The United States has the highest standard of living in the world, and much of this is due to the effectiveness of our work organizations. A major change in the way our work organizations are managed carries with it some enormous risks. Nevertheless, it may be even riskier to not change, to continue to manage as we always have. So many factors argue for change that to not change is to assure obsolescence.

Origin of Traditional Approaches

Much of the detail of managing manufacturing organizations in the United States was provided by the work of Frederick Winslow Taylor around the turn of the century (*The Principles of Scientific Management*, 1911). Taylor, the father of modern industrial engineering, emphasized that the work of lower-level participants in organizations should be specialized, standardized, and simplified. He went on to stress the advantages of machine pacing and limited, carefully written job definitions. Authority and decision making were supposed to rest at the top while the lower-level participants were asked to focus on doing, not thinking. Thinking, coordinating, and controlling were left to management. This approach to designing work ultimately resulted in the assembly line and its tremendous productivity gains.

In many respects the assembly line and the concepts of Frederick Winslow Taylor were ready-made for an American work force that was made up of poorly educated immigrants who, in many cases, did not speak English. Thus, the idea of work that required doing, but not thinking, was quite appropriate. Research was not done to "prove" that this was the right way to manage; it simply made sense and thus was widely adopted.

For decades after Taylor's original work the United States dominated worldwide thinking about how organizations should be managed. Many American firms were seen as models of effective management (for example, General Motors and American Telephone and Telegraph). During the fifties and sixties there even seemed to be a fear on the part of many Europeans that because of their managerial skills American organizations would dominate world markets. In the late 1960s a book about the dominance and effectiveness of American management was a best-seller in Europe (*The American Challenge*, Servan-Schreiber, 1968), just as in the early 1980s a book about Japanese management was a best-seller in the United States (*Theory Z*, Ouchi, 1981).

For a while it seemed as if American managers had discovered the ultimate approach to management: a combination of careful controls, centralized top-down decision making, and carefully programmed and prescribed tasks for production employees. In short, separate thinking from doing and concentrate expertise, decision-making power, and information at the higher levels of organizations, where highly trained managers can make the decisions.

Criticism Begins

Criticisms of the traditional approach to managing work organizations in the United States are not new. Starting in the 1950s, writers such as Argyris, McGregor, and Likert emphasized the negative social consequences of the management methods of many U.S. corporations. They talked about the debilitating consequences of giving people simplified, standardized jobs and the negative effect that this has on employees' motivation for productivity and for doing high-quality work. They talked, but few listened.

In retrospect, it is hardly surprising that little change took place. There was no reason to change: the United States was at the zenith of its economic power. During this period managers took a "show me" approach. They wanted proof that participative management practices were superior to their current management practices, proof that was very hard to come by in the absence of organizations willing to try implementing such practices. Managers also tended to overlook the fact that their current operating methods had never been proven to be best. But that was not the point—the point was that current operations were successful. A new approach involves risk as well as unlearning an old method and learning a new one. Change occurs only when there is a compelling reason to change.

Initial Experiments Begin

During the 1950s and 1960s some pioneering work in the area of job enrichment was done at American Telephone and Telegraph (AT&T) and other companies. It involved expanding jobs so that employees would have more responsibility and authority. At the same time the writings of McGregor, Argyris, and others became required reading in most business schools. Widespread change, however, did not occur. Instead participative management was treated as an interesting academic theory that stimulated debate on how work should be designed. All too frequently this debate focused in a nonproductive way on whether people really wanted interesting, challenging work or whether they preferred to do boring repetitive jobs. Some individuals argued that the advantages of uninvolving work included the opportunity to think about off-the-job activities and to have an exciting personal and social life. Those who favored participation pointed to attitude survey data which showed that people wanted more interesting work.

I remember all too well one debate I had with Mitchell Fein, an industrial engineer who later invented a gainsharing plan that will be discussed later. He argued that less than 20 percent of the workforce want participation; he called me unrealistic and uninformed and pointed out that I did not really understand workers. I suggested that he was advocating an outdated and ineffective view of work. I doubt if any of the forty company presidents who listened changed their minds as a result of this debate. Interestingly, a few did seem to change their minds at the same session when Gordon Zachs, the president of R. G. Barry Corporation, advocated participative management. I learned a valuable lesson from this session about the relative ability of academics and executives to influence the opinions of managers.

As the 1970s began, little change was occurring in the way organizations were managed in the United States. Two important national initiatives were launched to change this. The Department of Health, Education, and Welfare under Elliot Richardson commissioned the writing of a major report ultimately published as a book titled *Work in America* (1973). It made a strong and passionate argument for changing the nature of bureaucratic organizations in the United States. It also set off a highly visible national debate around the type of work that people prefer and the impact of work design on people's productivity and well-being. No ultimate conclusion was reached, but the book sensitized people to the alternatives to organizations in which information, power, rewards, and knowledge are concentrated at the top. The book also pointed out that jobs that are based on the principles of simplification, standardization, and specialization may have potentially significant negative consequences for society, including poor mental health, alcoholism, lack of personal growth and development, poor work quality, poor attendance, and high turnover rates.

Also in the early 1970s, important initiatives to encourage experimentation with joint union-management quality-of-work-life projects began. The largest company program was started by General Motors. A large multi-company/union project was started by the Institute for Social Research at the University of Michigan and the National Quality of Work Center in Washington, D.C. These organizations, funded partially by the Ford Foundation and the Department of Commerce, started eight carefully studied experiments in union-management cooperation.

During this same period, several companies, most notably Procter & Gamble and General Foods, built new design plants that incorporated important new approaches to work design and management (Lawler, 1978). These will be discussed later, but it is important to note here that they, too, became part of the national debate about how work organizations should be managed. In particular, the Topeka, Kansas, General Foods plant became the object of considerable press attention. The plant became so well known that it was able to charge visitors a fee for a tour and explanation of the management system. *Business Week,* the *Wall Street Journal,* and *Fortune* all wrote about it. Some said it was socialism, democracy gone wild, or worse yet, a form of communism. Others said it was the most effective management approach ever invented.

The reasons this plant generated such attention and strong feelings are important. It moved beyond the experiments in job design; changes occurred in the work of lower-level employees as well as in some fundamental features of the management system. The emphasis was on moving information, power, rewards, and knowledge to the lowest levels. When this became obvious to managers elsewhere in the United States, it significantly challenged them. When it became obvious to higher-level managers in General Foods, it produced quite a case of indigestion. They ultimately decided they were not happy with the situation there and replaced a number of the managers.

Overall, the early 1970s was a period of experimentation, learning, and most of all, debate about the effectiveness of different approaches to management. However, those who argued for change in management style had reason to be discouraged. It seemed as if the traditional bureaucratic approach to managing work organizations had again survived a challenge to its basic premises. Once again critics questioned whether people really wanted more involving work and whether organizations

like the Topeka General Foods plant were in fact more effective. (A study I did suggested it was about 40 percent more
effective than a comparable plant.) Many of the people associated with work restructuring and experimentation were seen
as do-gooders who had a poor sense of what it takes to create an
effective work organization.

Forces for Change in the 1980s

At this point in the eighties, the negativism of the late
seventies has been reversed. Once again the momentum is working for those who argue for abandoning the traditional model.
For a major social change to take place the mere existence of a
new approach is not enough: there must be a recognized need
for change and a reason to change (Mohrman and Lawler, 1985).
Until recently there was no compelling reason to change. American organizations were admired worldwide. American businesses
were seen as threatening to dominate the economies of many of
our European trading partners. A dramatic change has occurred,
however. Many Americans now perceive our slow growth in productivity and poor managerial performance as a threat to our
economic well-being.

Survey data from the Opinion Research Corporation
(O'Boyle, 1985) show a decided decline in the percent of employees who favorably rate their companies and managements.
For example, among hourly employees the favorable rating
toward management has dropped from about 40 percent in
1975-1979 to just over 20 percent in 1980-1984. Robert Reich
(1985), in a highly critical article, has argued that by almost any
measure America's top corporations have performed poorly
over the last fifteen years. According to Reich, they have lost
markets and have experienced waning productivity, poor quality, and a lower rate of innovation. Since 1970 the net profits
of America's largest corporations have declined 20 percent
when adjusted for inflation. Reich adds that a major cause of
this "abysmal" situation is concentration of power and rewards
in the hands of top management.

In summary, changes are needed in the way American organizations are managed. My belief is that in most situations some form of participative management represents the best answer. This belief is based on a combination of some important social trends and some realities about how organizations operate; the next two chapters explore these trends and realities.

2

Why Participative Approaches Meet Today's Needs

Approaches to organizing and managing are not inherently effective or ineffective. They are effective to the degree that they fit existing conditions. To be effective a management approach needs to fit the existing societal values, the nature of the work force, the type of product being produced, and the business environment. Because all of these factors determine the effectiveness of a management approach, its effectiveness may change over time. For example, the traditional bureaucratic style based on the kind of industrial engineering model presented by Taylor could be expected to be quite effective for decades but might lose its effectiveness as a result of changes in the society and the work force. Similarly, in countries with different cultures, very different management approaches may be called for. In short, there is no one correct style. The crucial thing is to develop and practice a style that fits the conditions at a given point in time.

In the United States it is striking how much those factors that determine the effectiveness of a management style have changed during the last forty to fifty years (see Kerr and Rosow, 1979; also Naisbitt, 1982; Naisbitt and Aburdene, 1985; and O'Toole, 1981, for reviews). The society, the work force, the

12

products produced, and the business environment that exist in the United States are all dramatically different from those that existed at the turn of the century and even through World War II. Let us briefly review how the situation has changed. This will point out why there is currently such receptivity to new approaches to management and will also establish what kind of new management style will be effective in today's environment.

Business Environment

Undoubtedly the major reason why organizations are more receptive to new approaches is the changing nature of the business environment in the United States. For the first time we find ourselves losing in productivity and quality to international competitors. As was pointed out earlier, effecting major social change requires a recognized need to change. In recent years the international competitive business environment has provided that need.

Because the manufacturing and marketing of products such as automobiles, steel, and electronics have spread to other nations, American organizations find themselves competing with organizations in other countries that practice quite different, and in some cases highly effective, approaches to managing. General Motors is a good case in point. For decades "all" they had to do to be effective was to perform better than other U.S. auto makers. They usually did this and, as a result, were regarded as a leading example of how to manage a large organization (O'Toole, 1985). The high wages they paid their employees for doing simple, repetitive jobs and the adversarial relationship they had with their union did not put them at a disadvantage because their competition had the same problems. This changed dramatically when the Japanese entered the market with a different approach to management. Although not as well publicized, Xerox experienced similar problems in the copier business that they created, as did Kodak in the film business that they pioneered.

The tough international competition provided by Japan and others has been particularly difficult for U.S. companies, given the slow rate of productivity growth in the United States. Since 1970, Japanese productivity has more than doubled, while that of the United States has increased by less than 50 percent. France and Germany have increased their productivity by more than 75 percent over the same period. A point to remember is that U.S. organizations are still the most productive in the world. However, this lead has been shrinking for decades and unless growth significantly increases within the near future, it may disappear entirely.

As is shown in Table 1, our labor costs are the highest in the world. Japan's, for example, are only 51 percent of ours, while we are only slightly more productive. Given the labor cost disadvantage, American organizations need to be much more productive in order to be competitive.

Table 1. Labor Costs as a Percentage of U.S. Costs in 1983.

West Germany	84
Netherlands	78
Sweden	73
France	62
Italy	62
Britain	53
Japan	51
Brazil	14
Taiwan	13
Mexico	12
South Korea	10

Source: Bureau of Labor Statistics.

In the United States not only is labor expensive, so is capital. New plants, equipment, and offices do not come cheap in an environment where interest rates are high. Given the high cost of labor and the expense of labor-saving equipment, it is particularly important that labor be productive. The very survival of some American industries depends on effectively utilizing labor, which, in turn, depends on how people are organized and managed.

Products and Technology

During the last several decades the U.S. economy has shifted toward a service orientation and toward work requiring specialized knowledge. According to Labor Department statistics, the percentage of the work force in blue collar occupations dropped from 36.6 percent in 1960 to 28.5 percent in 1985, while service workers increased from 18.6 percent to 25.5 percent. Most approaches to organization and management are based on the industrial production model. That model was fine when the U.S. economy was heavily concentrated in manufacturing, but this is no longer true. The major economic growth is now in the service sector: this has produced an increasing number of jobs in which people are working with words, symbols, numbers, and personal services.

Banks, insurance companies, hospitals, engineering firms, and similar organizations represent an increasingly large percentage of workplaces in the United States. In many cases machine pacing and the kind of industrial engineering concepts that were so effectively applied to manufacturing simply do not fit. Machine pacing, simplification, and standardization can still be applied to a degree (although they are often misapplied in banks, insurance companies, and other paper-processing mills); however, much more of the work is under employee control, and the effectiveness of the employee is much less observable by a traditional supervisor. The same thing, interestingly, is true of highly automated manufacturing environments and high-technology firms. More workers are needed who can repair complex machinery, think for themselves, solve problems, and make decisions. This is particularly true in such process production facilities as chemical plants, oil refineries, food processing plants, and others.

In short, in many U.S. organizations, employees are the critical resource. They are more important than the physical assets of the organization. People Express Airline symbolizes this by calling its people hard assets and its planes soft assets. This is in notable contrast to the typical work organizations of earlier decades. There the physical assets were the key and the management style reflected this.

Work Force Changes

Changes in the U.S. work force in the last several decades have been dramatic, multifaceted, and important. It is beyond the scope of this chapter to review all of them in depth (see, for example, Kerr and Rosow, 1979; Rosow, 1981; Yankelovich, 1983). It is important, however, to mention a few changes that have direct implications for the way in which people will respond to different management styles.

Perhaps the most important change has been the increasing level of education in society. More and more people are finishing high school, going to college, and enrolling in continuing education programs. The result is that today's work force is educationally much different from the one that existed just ten to twenty years ago. In 1964, 45.1 percent of the work force had high school diplomas; in 1984, Labor Department statistics indicate it was 59.7 percent. A recent census bureau report revealed that 86 percent of today's twenty-five- to twenty-nine-year-olds have a high school diploma, making Americans the most educated people in the world. In addition, people have developed expectations that they will be able to use the knowledge and education that they obtained in school and often view their education as time invested in obtaining a better job (Lawler, 1985; O'Toole, 1977, 1981).

There is also considerable evidence that the population is less willing to take orders simply because they are given by somebody in authority. This is undoubtedly tied into the increasing level of education and is terribly important because of its strong conflict with traditional approaches to management, which often rest on the assumption that people will take orders simply because they are given by somebody with greater authority. For decades this was true in the United States, but now workers seem to be increasingly challenging orders given by people who are in positions of traditional authority or who have what is often called "position power." This is particularly true when those people do not have the commensurate expertise to back up those orders. Some observe that we are now in a society in which authority derives from expertise more than from positions (see, for example, Bennis and Nanus, 1985). There is also evidence that managers are becoming less willing to give orders. Data collected by Doug Bray, former director of AT&T's research program on managerial effectiveness, shows that younger managers have fewer needs for dominance as well as for deferring to authority. In other words they are less interested both in ordering and in being ordered.

Tied in with the willingness of people to challenge traditional authority figures is an increased concern about due process and employee rights. Employees are increasingly conscious of their legal and societal rights to have a say in decisions and to challenge what they perceive to be unfair and arbitrary decision making on the part of management. To a degree this may represent nothing more than a spilling over of our societal values into the workplace. The American society is one that aspires to freedom of speech, democracy, and "one person, one vote" (Ewing, 1977, 1983).

Table 2 shows data on employees' attitudes about the kind of influence they would like to have on organizational decisions (Lawler, Renwick, and Bullock, 1981). As the data show, employees would like to have significantly more influence than they currently have in a number of areas. Particularly important here is the fact that individuals want a strong influence on how they do their work. This argues strongly for participative approaches that push decisions, information, and knowledge about day-to-day work activities to the lowest levels in organizations.

Other important changes in the work force include the significant entry of minorities and women, the arrival of immigrant groups, and the entry of the baby boom generation into the workplace. However, the most important changes for management style are those concerned with education and the desire of employees to have a say in the events and decisions that affect their lives. This particular trend is in direct contrast to the traditional bureaucratic approaches to organizing and

Table 2. Employees' Responses to Questions About Their Influence.
N = 2,300

	Actually Have Influence (Mean)	Should Have Influence (Mean)	Mean Difference (Should-Actual)
How to do own work	5.7	6.2	0.5
Schedule own work	5.3	5.9	0.6
Giving pay raises	2.1	3.8	1.7
Hiring people	2.6	3.7	1.1
Firing people	2.5	3.6	1.1
Promoting people	2.3	3.5	1.2
Making organizational policy	2.9	4.5	1.6

Note: 1 = No say; 7 = A great deal of say.

managing work that do not give power, knowledge, rewards, and information to most employees.

In summary, the new work force is more entitlements oriented, and it feels that it is entitled to such things as good jobs, fair wages, good benefits, and a say in decision making, things that previous generations might have felt they had to earn (O'Toole, 1981). Because of this change, the old way of managing, which assumes that people will accept a system in which a limited number of people slowly earn power and rewards and gain access to information, is no longer acceptable.

Societal Changes

Perhaps the most important societal change that affects management style is the extensive legislation enacted to protect employee rights. Age, sex, and race discrimination laws make it increasingly important for organizations to deal with people fairly. Dissatisfied employees can find recourse through the courts if they feel unfairly affected by almost any important decision that an organization makes about them (Ewing, 1983). Thus, it is becoming increasingly important for organizations to manage people in a way that is generally considered fair and reasonable. It also means that the cost of poor human resource management is high. Specifically, it means that it is no longer acceptable for a manager to simply say, "You're fired because I say you're fired." Dismissals, lack of pay increases, and other negative actions have to be backed up by careful preparation and well-documented performance records.

For decades society somehow exempted work organizations from the mandate that things be democratic, participative, and egalitarian. People accepted without challenge the idea that they should vote on who is going to be president of the United States and who is going to set their taxes but that they should have little say in who their supervisor is or in who the president of their company is. Indeed, people were quite willing to give up their constitutional and democratic rights when they entered the workplace (Ewing, 1983; *Work in America*, 1973). There is increasing evidence, however, that this attitude is changing. People are becoming less comfortable with a society in which work organizations are autocratic while the political and other features of their lives are democratic. One of the reasons for this societal change is undoubtedly an increasing awareness that work organizations can be effectively managed in a democratic and participative manner.

Participative Management: The Best Answer

The societal, business, product, and work force changes that have occurred argue strongly for a change in management style. Clearly, American organizations need to be more effective simply to be competitive—and not just somewhat more effective, but dramatically better. It is unlikely that dramatic improvements can come about through the use of traditional management approaches. It is very unlikely that research breakthroughs are going to tell us how to make the traditional approaches to management operate more effectively. Certainly, they can be better executed than they typically are, but it is hard to believe that better execution will lead to the kind of improvement that is needed. This kind of improvement seems much more likely to come from a new approach than from simply doing the old better. But what new approach? My reading of the trends suggests that some form of participative management makes the most sense because it fits well with the major changes.

Participative management suits the current work force, technologies, and societal conditions better than any other alternative. In addition, as we shall see in the next chapter, there is reason to believe it can produce improvements in areas where they are badly needed, such as product quality and labor costs. They have been very effective in some cases. This is particularly encouraging because it offers the possibility of further gains in organizational effectiveness and employee well-being as we learn more about how to manage in a participative way.

3

Participation and Organizational Effectiveness

Employee participation is an attractive idea, especially from the perspective of societal values. However, it is important to look separately at values and organizational effectiveness. Chapter Two argues that employee participation can significantly improve organizational effectiveness. Now we need to review some of the rationale for this argument, including research on this topic. This will acquaint readers with some basic findings and prepare them to interpret the results produced by different approaches to participative management.

A significant amount of research has focused on how participation affects five major determinants of organizational effectiveness: motivation, satisfaction, acceptance of change, problem solving, and communication. We will review these issues and consider when and how participation might affect the financial performance of organizations. But before we do this, we need to identify the key characteristics of participative management.

Characteristics of Participative Approaches

There is a wide variety of programs and approaches that can enhance the level of employee participation in an organization. Participation is not something that organizations either have or do not have—it comes in many forms and can be brought about in many ways. The four elements of participation that have been discussed so far—power, information, knowledge, and rewards—can be used to describe any participative management program. But they are more than just a way to describe participative approaches. Their presence or absence at lower levels in the organization is crucial in determining how effective a participative management program is. One last feature is also important: the proportion or part of the total organization that is affected. Once we determine how much of an organization is affected by changes in power, rewards, information, and knowledge, we can analyze its impact.

These same elements should also be useful to anyone who wants to utilize a participative management program in his or her organization. They are useful in determining what has changed or will change. Once this determination has been made, attention can be turned to what results can be expected.

Power: Decision-Making Approach. Discussions about participative decision making often give the impression that decisions are either made in a participative or a nonparticipative manner. In fact there are a number of decision-making styles, which vary from being highly participative to being purely autocratic or top-down. In viewing any employee participation program it is important to identify the actual decision-making or power-allocation approach that is taken. The following list of approaches to decision making (adapted from Tannenbaum and Schmidt, 1958) is a good way of classifying decision styles:

- *Top-Down.* Top-level individuals in the organization make the decision and tell people at lower levels what the decision is.
- *Consultative.* People at the top levels make a tentative decision, announce it to the organization and ask for input.
- *Consultative-Upward Communication.* Individuals at the lower level of the organization are expected to propose ideas and potential decisions to higher levels, but the ultimate decision-making power is always held by people at the top.
- *Consensus.* Decisions are widely discussed in the organiza-

tion and considered final only when everyone agrees that it is the right decision.

- *Delegation with Veto.* Decisions are given to lower-level employees and they make the decisions as a matter of course. However, high-level managers retain the power to reject the decision and ask the lower-level people to look at it again.
- *Delegation with Policy Philosophy Guidelines.* Choices are given to lower-level employees and they make the decisions within certain constraints. Guidelines for decisions are often given that involve strategy, philosophy, or values.
- *Pure Delegation.* Decisions are given to the lower-level employees and they are free to make them in whatever way they wish.

The effects of each of these approaches are somewhat different and, depending on the decision to be made, any one of them may be the best style to use (Vroom and Yetton, 1973). Organizations make an enormous range of decisions. They vary from very high-level strategic decisions about finance and marketing to very routine day-to-day decisions about how a product or service is going to be delivered. It is rare for any of these decisions to be made by pure delegation. However there are examples of their being made by styles other than top-down. For example, in their new Saturn business, General Motors has agreed to discuss all these issues with the union. Recently the employees of a software firm, Multimate, voted on whether it should develop a new product line. In discussing any participative program, the first point to consider is how different types of decisions are going to be made. There is no well-developed classification system for describing different types of decisions but there are a few important distinctions.

One set of decisions that stands out from others is the type that involves the day-to-day conducting of business: rate of productivity, quality, work methods, procedures, and so on. These factors are relevant to everyone's job; job-holders usually have information about them and, as a number of studies have shown, a desire to influence them. Decisions concerning how the job is to be done can be made by the job-holder but often are made by the supervisor or by staff support individuals who are experts in financial information systems, work methods, engineering, and so forth. In many participative management programs, these decisions are delegated to work teams.

Distinguishable from day-to-day decisions are the higher-level strategy decisions. These involve how the organization will be structured and financed, the kinds of products or services it will offer, and the overall strategical and tactical issues that are involved in running the organization. In most organizations these decisions are made by top-level management.

Finally, there are a number of decisions that involve human resource management. These include decisions regarding pay, staffing, promotion, training, and other issues that affect individual careers and rewards. These decisions are typically made by a combination of the personnel department and top management, but of course, they need not be. In some participative management approaches they are made by the employees at the lowest level. In a number of plants where I have worked as a consultant, salary, hiring, and promotion decisions are made by the employees. One plant recently needed to lay off a small number of employees. After some hesitation the decision was made to delegate this decision to the production employees. They made the decision without using the crutch of seniority— they focused on contribution. It was not easy, however, and many tears were shed (literally) as peers evaluated each other and worked through the decision process. As we will see in discussing participative program elements, such as quality circles and job enrichment, participative programs vary substantially both in decision style and in the kind of decisions they involve.

Information. Information is at the very core of what makes a group of people an organization (Lawler and Rhode, 1976). It is a source of power and effectiveness in organizational coordination and cooperation. Without considerable information moving downward, employee participation and involvement become impractical and even dangerous. It is therefore crucial in employee involvement programs that certain kinds of information be moved to lower levels (Cole, 1985).

In considering the different participative programs, we

will focus on how the downward information flow in the organization is changed. Specifically, the focus will be on such questions as: Is new information provided to production workers? What kind of information is sent downward in the organization? And what access do people at all levels have to financial information?

The downward flow of information in organizations is only half the story; the other half, of course, is the upward flow. Information concerning improvement ideas, performance, and employee attitudes sometimes does not flow upward in organizations. Every approach to participative management tries to assure a good upward flow of information. Many companies use attitude surveys to assure that employee opinions are well-known to top management. At Kodak, for example, monthly trend data are reported to top management. Just as a good downward flow of information is required for organizational effectiveness, so is a good upward flow. Without it, coordination and utilization of employee ideas is virtually impossible.

Regarding information flow in organizations, both the kinds of information and how individuals can get access to the information are important. Participative management approaches focus on such information as ideas for improvement, employee attitudes, operating results, strategic plans, and performance of competitors. Because there may be a significant difference between the flow of information concerning ideas and the flow of information concerning financial results, these need to be looked at separately when considering the impact of participative management approaches.

Access to information can differ substantially. For example, the individual may be in an area that has a computer terminal which allows direct access to the data. An example of less direct communication flow is when an individual has to ask for specific data from people in higher-level positions or in other parts of the organization. Finally, there is the situation where the individual's only access to information is general announcements or printed materials that are distributed as a matter of course in the regular information system of the organization.

Rewards. Rewards are important determinants of behavior

in organizations (Lawler, 1981). As such they are an important consideration in any participative program. Both intrinsic (internal) rewards and extrinsic (external) rewards can be affected by participative programs. Such intrinsic rewards as feelings of accomplishment and self-worth can be increased as a result of individuals being involved in important work decisions.

Participation also raises a number of issues concerning such extrinsic rewards as pay and promotion. As people obtain more power, information, and knowledge they expect more rewards, particularly when they feel their participation has made the organization more effective (Mohrman and Lawler, 1985). As we shall see, some participative programs take this into account. They provide rewards for increased organizational effectiveness and argue that economic participation needs to be combined with participation in decisions. By sharing the gains they add another facet to employee participation. Other programs build in higher salaries for individuals as they acquire more knowledge. In order to understand the impact of a participative management program we must consider how rewards are distributed in general and in particular whether lower-level employees are rewarded on the basis of organizational performance. Basing rewards on organizational performance is particularly desirable because it aligns employees' interests with organizational effectiveness.

Knowledge and Skills. At the core of any effort to involve employees in an organizational decision is their expertise and knowledge regarding the decision and the operation of the organization in general. Again, participative programs vary widely in the degree to which they provide training and develop people's knowledge as part of the participative program.

If training is involved, it is important to look at the kind of training that is done. It can cover such topics as interpersonal skills, problem analysis and decision-making skills, economic education to help employees understand their business unit, education in the operation of the organization, and a wide array of technical training that may either be directly related to the individual's job or related to the broader running of the organization.

Obviously there is a big difference between training individuals in how to do their own jobs better (including relevant technical skills) and training them in group and interpersonal skills, leadership skills, and the economics of the business. The latter enables individuals to participate in a much broader array of decision-making activities and affects their expectations about the kinds of decisions and activities in which they will be involved.

How Much of the Organization? Participative programs differ in the amount of the organization they affect. Some affect only a few individuals or work groups, while others affect whole plants and corporations. Some corporations, such as Honeywell, Cummins Engine, Xerox, and Motorola, have stated that their goal is to have corporate-wide employee participation efforts. Other organizations, such as General Electric, have simply installed participative work groups within existing plants. At AT&T, jobs were redesigned to give individuals more latitude and input about how their work is done. Quality circles are another example of an approach that affects only a few individuals at a time, since participation in them is usually limited to only a small part of the work force.

In examining participative programs it is very important to consider how much of an organization is affected. There is good reason to believe that this is a crucial factor in determining how effective a participative program will be and how long it will survive. Results of a number of studies have shown that programs that are limited to a few individuals or a few groups often have trouble surviving because they are foreign entities in an environment that is hostile to them (see, for example, Goodman, 1979). As a result, they often succumb to pressures to be like everyone else even though they have some initial success. From its inception the Topeka plant of General Foods, mentioned earlier, was subject to strong pressures to be more like the rest of the corporation. During my work there, several key managers were dismissed because they were unwilling to manage in the "General Foods way," this despite evidence that the plant was quite successful.

Key Questions. Employee participation raises a number

of very complex issues. It is practically impossible to say anything about the potential effectiveness of a program or about its nature from merely knowing that it is called an employee participation program. An adequate description of such a program requires information concerning five areas:

1. The type of decision-making changes that are instituted.
2. The type of knowledge that is developed in the work force.
3. The way in which rewards are affected.
4. The way in which the upward and downward flow of information is affected.
5. How much of the organization is involved.

Only when this range of issues is considered can the program be accurately described and reasonable predictions made about its success. As we shall see next, simply having people involved in decision making will not automatically lead to increased productivity and organizational effectiveness.

Participation and Motivation

The relationship between participation and motivation is complex (Vroom, 1964). In order to adequately discuss it, a few words of background are needed regarding motivation. Motivation is a result of people's beliefs about the consequences of their actions (Lawler, 1973; Pinder, 1984). People are motivated to perform an action when they perceive that the consequences of the action are favorable to them; that is, when they perceive that they will achieve goals or outcomes that they desire. In most situations individuals are faced with a number of possible behaviors. At work, for example, they can choose to perform at many different levels of effectiveness. Given a choice, people behave in the way they think has the most favorable results.

The writings of Maslow (1954) and others on the nature of human needs are relevant to understanding individuals' desires. They point out that individuals have multiple needs, some of which can be satisfied by such extrinsic rewards as pay, recognition from the boss, recognition from other people, and security. They also stress that individuals have intrinsic needs for such things as personal growth and accomplishment. These needs can be satisfied by internal rewards, such as feelings of personal growth, accomplishment, and self-fulfillment. The distinction between intrinsic and extrinsic rewards is very important. Intrinsic rewards have to be given by the individual to himself or herself; all the organization can do is set up conditions where this is possible. Extrinsic rewards, such as money and promotion, can be formally allocated by an organization.

Motivation theory emphasizes that it is people's perception of a situation that is crucial. Reality affects perception but people act directly on the basis of their perceptions. Thus individuals must see connections between their performance and rewards if performance motivation is to be present. Time after time I find that managers miss this crucial point. They assume that because they see a relationship between rewards, like pay, and performance that their subordinates do. When I research the situation I often find that there is a relationship but because of poor communication and low trust, it is not perceived: the result—no motivation.

One final note is important with respect to motivation. Unless individuals perceive that the behavior or performance that leads to a valued reward is achievable, they will not be motivated to perform. Thus an organization may clearly tie a number of very positive rewards to a particular level of performance and still find that individuals are not motivated to perform at that level simply because they do not perceive that they can achieve the performance. This point is also missed by a number of managers. They set "stretch" goals for their employees to assure that they will strive to do their best. In doing this they often set goals that are so high that the subordinates perceive they have no chance of reaching them: the result—no motivation.

In summary, motivation theory suggests that people will be motivated to perform well when three conditions exist:

1. Rewards are perceived to be tied to performance.

2.   The rewards that are tied to performance are valued.
3.   Effective performance is perceived to be achievable.

Research shows that participation in decisions can affect motivation, however, it is not a straightforward relationship. First, it depends on people's needs for control, competence, achievement, self-fulfillment, and personal growth. It is these needs that are satisfied by participation. The participative process makes it possible for employees to obtain rewards that satisfy these needs. It is because of this relationship that the debate about people's needs is relevant to the issue of whether participative management is likely to be effective.

Perhaps the most direct relationship between motivation and participation occurs when people participate in setting goals and commit themselves to achieving these goals. According to research, when people participate in setting goals and get information about their performance two things happen. First, they set goals that are perceived by them to be achievable. Second, their sense of self-esteem and competence becomes tied to achieving the goals and therefore they are highly motivated to achieve them (see, for example, Locke and Latham, 1984). In short, participation has the effect of stimulating or creating a connection between a particular level of performance and the reception of intrinsic rewards. This means that participation in goal setting can have a significant impact on motivation.

The key here is that the participation must concern an important work performance issue in order for it to affect motivation. One clear implication is that giving people a say in such issues as how the parking lots will be laid out, when the softball games will be played, how the recreation money will be spent, and so on, may have no impact on their motivation to perform their job well. Only participation in work performance decisions is likely to affect performance motivation.

I still remember very clearly a call I received about ten years ago. It was from an auto plant manager who wanted "advice" on participation. He wanted to paint part of his plant and he wanted to know if he should give employees the chance to choose a color for their machines. He had already narrowed the choices to three (red, white, and blue—it was the time of the bicentennial) but he was concerned that the employees could not be trusted to choose among the three. My advice to him was that he could get in real trouble by giving them a choice, not because they could not choose wisely as he feared but because they might be insulted by the trivial nature of the choice.

Participation can also have an impact on motivation through a process that has been studied extensively with respect to job design. (Chapters Six and Seven review this work.) When people are given interesting tasks, participation in decisions about how to perform the tasks, and feedback about performance, intrinsic motivation is high. It is high because people feel responsible for how well the work is performed. As a result, they become intrinsically motivated to perform it well. Such rewards as self-esteem, self-fulfillment, and a sense of competence get tied to how well it is performed. Quality is the key here; people become motivated to do high-quality work. They want to be associated with a high-quality product because this satisfies their needs for competence and self-esteem.

Participation in the financial success of an organization can also have a direct, strong impact on motivation. If money is important to the work force, and if there is a clear connection between pay and performance, money will be a motivator. Although it seems like it should be simple to use financial participation as a motivator, it is often difficult (Lawler, 1973). There are, however, some interesting examples of how this can be done and these will be reviewed in Chapter Nine, which deals with gainsharing plans.

In summary then, research suggests that participation can affect motivation under certain conditions. Specifically, when people participate in decisions about target performance levels and goals, it can affect their commitment to achieving those goals. It can also affect motivation to produce a high-quality product or service when people are given some say in how the work is to be done, what methods are to be used, and how their day-to-day work activities are to be carried out. Finally, financial rewards can have a direct impact on motivation if they are important and are tied to performance in ways that employees can understand and influence.

Satisfaction and Participation

It is easy to confuse the concepts of motivation and satisfaction, as do some of the writings on participation. They assume that participation will automatically affect both motivation and satisfaction and suggest that they are closely related, if not synonymous. They are, in fact, very different. Motivation is influenced by forward-looking perceptions concerning the relationship between performance and rewards, while satisfaction refers to people's feelings about the rewards they have received. Thus, satisfaction is a consequence of past events while motivation is a consequence of their expectations about the future. People's expectations about the future are at least partially based on the past, but they are not completely determined by them.

Research rather clearly shows that satisfaction and motivation are not closely related (Vroom, 1964). Thus, it is quite possible for people to be very satisfied with their jobs but not particularly motivated to perform them well. Over the years I have studied a number of organizations that practice "country club" management. They place few demands on their employees, pay them well, and treat them with respect and dignity. In short, they do everything for the employees but typically get low performance because they neither reward high performance nor demand it.

Satisfaction is clearly related to one type of work behavior—the willingness of individuals to continue as employees of an organization and to show up for work on a regular basis. The reason for this is rather straightforward. When people have a satisfying relationship with the organization they work for, they perceive it is to their advantage to continue to be a member of the organization. This does not mean that people who are satisfied will necessarily be good performers. It simply means that their membership is likely to continue.

When people have needs for control, participation, self-esteem, and self-fulfillment, then the opportunity to participate in decisions and control their own work leads to higher levels of satisfaction. The evidence suggests that the absence of participation can be a serious cause of dissatisfaction and that organizations that do not provide these opportunities may find themselves with high rates of absenteeism and rapid turnover. Considerable research shows that both absenteeism and turnover can be very expensive for an organization. For example, turnover often costs anywhere from five to twenty-five times an employee's monthly salary (Mirvis and Lawler, 1984; Flamholtz, 1974). Obviously, if turnover can be reduced, the cost of training, recruiting, poor performance on the part of new employees, and overstaffing due to people learning new jobs can also be reduced.

Similarly, absenteeism can be particularly costly for organizations. It often leads to overstaffing, assigning people to jobs they do not know how to do, and of course, discipline and its associated cost.

Absenteeism and turnover are not equally expensive for all organizations. Organizations in which the jobs are simple and repetitive and in which people are easily replaced may not suffer as greatly as others. Fast-food restaurants, for example, with their simple, easily learned jobs, are designed to reduce the cost of absenteeism and turnover. Thus, whether the increased satisfaction that can stem from participation will lead to a financial payback for the organization depends on the kind of work done as well as on the employees who work there.

Resistance to Change

Evidence shows that participation in decisions about major organizational changes can lead to a significant reduction in resistance to change (Coch and French, 1949). The problem of resistance to change is a fundamental and pervasive one in most organizations because of the rapid changes in today's society and the consequent need for organizations to change. All too often organizations find that change is difficult because it is not embraced by employees. Participation clearly represents a potential approach to overcoming resistance.

At least three processes seem to go on when people participate in change. One is a motivational process that is related to people becoming psychologically committed to installing the change. When people participate in designing a change and they decide that it is desirable, their intrinsic rewards and sense of self-esteem become tied to the successful implementation of that change. As a result, they are motivated to see that the change is successfully implemented and even that it is successful once it is implemented. This point is consistent with our earlier discussion of motivation and the way in which people are motivated to meet goals that they participate in setting.

The second process concerns how the nature of the change may be affected by participation. When people participate, they structure the change to be desirable to them; thus, the perceived consequences of the change on their work-day lives is positive. In the absence of participation, people often do not want some features of the change or do not understand the change and, as a result, perceive it as a negative event, even when it is not.

Communication is a third area in which participation can reduce resistance to change. More communication can aid acceptance by producing better understanding of the change. Of course, this will only reduce resistance if the change is, for the most part, a favorable one for the individuals involved. Communication often comes up as an important issue in change, because in many cases people imagine that the change will have more negative impact on them than it is likely to. I have seen people misperceive the consequence of change, particularly in factory situations. This often happens when a new piece of equipment is being installed. If people are not involved in the decision they perceive it as a threat to their job security, even though it may in fact improve their job. Interestingly, this same traditional "factory problem" frequently occurs in offices when computers are installed.

In summary, it appears that when people are given a significant role in designing a change, the change will be accepted more readily and the resistance to it will be overcome. This does not mean, however, that the change will necessarily be of a higher quality. As we shall see, this depends on several factors.

Problem Solving and Participation

Employee involvement in decisions that affect their work situations can be an effective way for devising better work methods and for solving important problems. For this to be truly effective however, three conditions need to exist. First, employees need to be knowledgeable about the issues that they are devising solutions to. Second, the employees must be motivated to solve the problem in a way that is consistent with the best interests of the organization. And third, mechanisms must be set up to facilitate the implementation of the solutions.

Let us briefly review why each of these three factors is important in problem solving. It is not hard to see why knowledge and information about the issues being solved are important ingredients. When the issues concern a particular work area, the person doing the job often has the best knowledge of the work to be done and, therefore, has the relevant expertise to solve problems and improve work methods.

Problems may arise when issues are of broader scope than those concerning the individual's immediate job. In many organizations people do not know much about what occurs in other parts of the organization and, as a result, their solutions are often rather myopic. I still remember a comment made to me over ten years ago by a production worker in a sawmill. I asked him what he would like to learn as part of a participative management program. He responded that he would like to *see* what happens to the product when it leaves his work station. (A wall blocked his view and he was not allowed to watch coworkers on the other side.) Employees also often lack knowledge and information about costs, investment plans, and changes in organizational strategy. This can be a critical failing if these factors make the solutions that employees develop unnecessary or unreasonable. All too often I have seen cases in which employees developed "good solutions" only to find out that they were beyond the existing investment guidelines or not needed because the product was being changed or phased out.

Individuals often lack the problem-solving skills needed to identify valid solutions and to develop arguments for their implementation. They also often lack the skills to sell their idea. In addition, they may lack critical group skills that are needed in the problem-solving process. It is therefore crucial to check on the degree to which the relevant skills and information are present.

Employees may not be motivated to devise a solution that is in the best interest of the organization. Good solutions could mean the elimination of their job, the interesting components of their work, or someone else's job. Therefore, organizations need to be very aware of the degree to which the participative process might ask for decisions that are not in employees' best interests.

When an issue might require a decision that is counter to a person's best interests, then it is necessary to change the organizational situation so that this is not true. Organizations can institute policies and practices that will do this. We shall discuss these further in Chapters Nine and Ten. The important point here is that only if this is done can the participative process produce solutions that are in the best interest of the organization.

Many participative programs falter at the implementation stage. In complex interconnected organizations, it is not simply a matter of two or three people deciding that an idea is a good one, installing it, and having it operate successfully. Decisions often require input from multiple work groups as well as such staff groups as the engineering department, the accounting department, and so on. Convincing all of these people that an idea is a good one can be difficult, time consuming, and frustrating. Obviously, unless the participatively developed idea is actually implemented, there is no gain for the organization or the individuals. Indeed there is likely to be a net decrement. Individuals tend to become cynical about the participative process and the organization has wasted time and effort in problem solving.

In summary, there is good reason to believe that employees can contribute significantly to a wide range of decisions when conditions are favorable. As we shall see in succeeding chapters, some programs do a good job of arranging conditions so that participation in problem solving will pay off for both the organization and the employees, but others do not.

Communication and Coordination

Taking part in problem solving, organizational policy setting, and work design can significantly increase employees' knowledge about the overall operation of the organization. This can facilitate coordination and communication among different work units, which can have a positive effect on those organizations in which significant levels of coordination and joint effort are required. Coordination and interdependency are critical issues in most of the organizations in our complex society, and thus the potential advantages of improving communication and coordination are significant.

One of the most important payoffs from allowing people to control their work and function in self-managing work teams is improved communication and coordination. Similarly, in problem-solving groups such as quality circles, people learn how other jobs are done and how to coordinate efforts to work together better.

For communication and coordination to improve as a result of a participative process, employees need to be trained and to have knowledge of the relevant issues. They need to have communication skills to interact effectively with others and also to be motivated to use the knowledge of how others function. The latter point is particularly important since without the motivation to use the information to make the organization more effective, the extra communication and knowledge are of little use.

Advantages and Disadvantages of Participation

There are clearly a number of potential advantages to a participative approach to management. These include higher motivation, satisfaction, better decision quality, and less resistance to change. These in turn can produce results that have a significant impact on organizational performance. The list below presents these potential payoff issues. In the remaining chapters we will look at a number of participative programs for improving organizational performance. In each case we will assess whether they produce the positive effects outlined in the following list.

- *Work Methods and Procedures.* Less resistance to new methods may result, and the problem-solving process may produce innovations.
- *Attraction and Retention of Employees.* Improvement results from increased satisfaction and involvement.
- *Staffing Flexibility.* Increased flexibility results from cross training and team work.
- *Service and Product Quality.* Higher motivation and better methods increase quality.
- *Rate of Output.* Higher motivation and better methods increase the rate of output.
- *Staff Support Level.* More "self-management" and broader skills reduce the staff support level.
- *Supervision.* More "self-management" and broader skills reduce the need for supervision.
- *Grievances.* Better communication and an improved union-management relationship reduce the number of grievances.
- *Decision-Making Quality.* Better input and decision-making processes improve the quality of decisions.
- *Skill Development.* Problem-solving as well as technical skills are developed.

The potential negative consequences of participation are listed below.

- *Salary Costs.* Developing new skills and responsibilities for lower-level participants results in increased salaries.
- *Training Costs.* If additional skills and knowledge are needed, training costs are increased.
- *Support Personnel.* If the new program creates a new structure that needs support and management, support personnel must increase.

- *Expectations for Organizational Change.* Any program that talks about participation increases expectations for organizational change. If the program is limited or fails, dissatisfaction and cynicism may result.
- *Resistance by Middle Management.* If middle management is not positively affected by the program, it may resist it.
- *Resistance by Staff Support Groups.* If staff support groups are not positively affected by the program, they may resist it.
- *Expectations for Personal Growth and Development.* If training and new experiences are part of the program expectations for personal growth and are not realized, frustration and dissatisfaction may result.
- *Lost Time.* Participation takes time and can slow decision making because a number of people have to understand and accept the decision.

This list is largely self-explanatory, given the discussion so far. Many of these costs are associated with the start-up of participative activities, while others result from the way in which the participative programs are designed and implemented.

We will test the approaches in the rest of the book against the above lists to determine their potential problems as well as their potential positive effects.

When Will Participation Work?

Much of the recent research and theory on organizations establishes that they can best be viewed as closely connected systems (see, for example, Nystrom and Starbuck, 1981). Thus, rather than being equal to the sum of their individual parts, they are only as effective as their ability to make their parts work together. A good analogy is an automobile engine. For an engine to work properly it is not sufficient to simply have the best carburetor, piston, block, and so on. The various components of the engine must fit with each other and complement each other. So it is with complex organizations that the various parts and design elements must fit with each other.

Current thinking about organizations identifies the following key features:

- *The Task It Intends to Perform.* This may be the delivery of a service or the manufacture of a product.
- *The Nature of the Individuals.* This includes their abilities, needs, and skills.
- *The Culture of the Organization.* This includes the beliefs of people about the right way to do things as well as their opinions about how things work in the organization.
- *The Formal Structure of the Organization.* This includes the reward system and the formal reporting relationships.

Most of the features of an organization are potentially changeable. People can be hired, trained, and fired, the structure can be altered, and so on. Culture is a somewhat different feature. Much recent writing on management has focused on culture and its importance, but little is known about how to change it (Peters and Waterman, 1982). To a degree, it is the product of the interaction of the other features of an organization, and thus to change it, other features have to be changed. The complication here is that often the existing culture makes it difficult to change other features of the organization. Chapter Twelve will explore in more detail what can be done to change organizations. I raise it now simply to stress the interconnectedness of organizations.

The organizational environment partially determines what is appropriate in terms of its systems or parts. That is, to be effective an organization needs to interface effectively with its environment. It must deliver goods and services to that environment and utilize the resources of the environment in order to survive. As was stressed in Chapter Two, it must also operate in ways that reflect the values, beliefs, and culture of the society.

The overall approach an organization takes in dealing with its environment is called its strategy. The various parts of the organization should be designed to support and implement the strategy that is selected.

Many issues of fit exist in organizational structuring. It is crucial, for example, that the reward system reward those behaviors that are consistent with the strategy. But this is not enough. The reward system must also fit with the types of jobs that exist, the individuals who work for the organization, and the reporting relationships in the structure. Major changes in the organization's task and strategy are particularly likely to raise crucial fit issues. If a change is made in the task an organization is doing (such as the change facing AT&T in going from a regulated utility to a competitive business), a change is typically required in the reward system, the reporting structure, and perhaps the individuals in the organization.

Often organizational ineffectiveness results because one feature of an organization is changed and the others are not changed to fit it. For example, simply changing the individuals in an organization may cause problems if the reward system, the tasks, and the structure are not changed as well. Similarly, if the structure is changed and the other parts are not, the resultant incongruence may cause serious problems.

The issue of fit and the systemic nature of organizations have some very important implications for the effectiveness of participative management approaches because these approaches change at least part of the formal structure. Decisions are moved lower in the organization and sometimes jobs are changed; this may necessitate changes in the other systems—for example, in the people, in the human resource management practices, and so on. Unless most systems in an organization are changed to be congruent with participative management practices, ultimately participative management programs will not be effective.

Changing only the nature of the jobs, for example, to allow participation may not be effective because it causes fit problems. Most organizations are designed for an autocratic approach to management, so all their components tend to be incongruent with participation. Thus, any change that involves participation should be assessed in terms of the breadth and depth of accompanying changes.

One factor may limit the effectiveness of participative management: the task the organization performs. If an organization has to perform a highly repetitive simple task, participative management may not fit. For example, I worked with a company that produces disposable medical products in large volumes. A major part of their work was wrapping thread around a packaging tab. A good worker can do hundreds per hour; the key to success was simply becoming machine-like. Similarly, most banks have individuals who encode checks at the rate of over a thousand an hour. Again, effectiveness depends on non-thinking repetition. Admittedly, these jobs could eventually be automated, but until they are it is hard to see how effectiveness can be improved by participative management. These tasks are the exception, but it is important to note that they continue to exist and that because of them participative management may not be appropriate in all situations.

Model of Effectiveness

A useful way to view the potential effectiveness of a participative program is to see how much it moves rewards, power, communication, and knowledge downward. Because congruence is important, it must move all of them in a similar way in order to be effective. If just one, two, or three of these key issues are affected, it leads to incongruence and ineffectiveness as the following examples illustrate:

- Power without knowledge, information, and rewards is likely to lead to poor decisions.
- Information and knowledge without power leads to frustration because people cannot use their expertise.
- Rewards for organizational performance without power, knowledge, and information lead to frustration and lack of motivation because people cannot influence their rewards.
- Information, knowledge, and power without rewards for organizational performance are dangerous because nothing will ensure that people will exercise their power in ways that will contribute to organizational effectiveness.

The congruence issue can be stated in terms of a simple equation. The degree to which an attribute is present at lower levels can be expressed on a 0-to-1 scale, with 0 meaning none of it is present and 1 a great deal is present. Rather than adding the amounts together, it is more appropriate to multiply the scores for each attribute, since we have argued that if one attribute is missing, the presence of the others is of limited value. This gives us the following equation:

Effectiveness of participative program = Rewards × Knowledge
X Power X
Information flow

In summary, my prediction is that for participative management to be effective, it must put power, rewards, knowledge, and an upward and downward information flow in place at the lower levels of an organization. Limited moves in this direction will, according to this view, produce limited or no results.

4

Quality Circles

The widespread adoption of quality circles has been called a revolution, a fad, a disaster, a key to making America productive again and last, but not least, a way to successfully compete with the Japanese. There may be doubt about the effectiveness of quality circles, but there is no doubt that they are being widely used in the United States at the present time.

As with any new approach to management, accurate data on the use of quality circles by American industry is lacking. Nevertheless, it seems clear that quality circles are operating in most *Fortune* 100 companies and probably most *Fortune* 500 companies. A New York Stock Exchange study in 1982 found that 65 percent of companies with over twenty-five thousand employees used quality-circle programs. The majority had started their programs within the previous two years, making quality circles the fastest-growing human resource activity. A 1984 Conference Board study (Gorlin and Schein, 1984) found that forty of fifty-two companies surveyed used them. Such corporations as Westinghouse and Honeywell have made major corporate commitments to quality circles in order to change their corporate cultures.

In just a few years, the United States has gone from a country with a few hundred people participating in quality circles to a country in which hundreds of thousands of workers are meeting regularly in quality circles. This phenomenon raises questions concerning why they are so popular, as well as questions about their effectiveness. Before we deal with these questions, we need to briefly discuss their history and characteristics.

History

Quality circles are not a new idea. Problem-solving groups like them have existed in the United States since the 1930s. Productivity improvement groups, which are part of many gain-sharing plans, strongly resemble quality circles. For decades there have been reports of the successful use of productivity improvement groups by such well-publicized companies as Donnelly Mirrors and Herman Miller.

The current popularity of quality circles in the United States can be traced directly to their widespread use in Japan, where much of their development was due to the early work of Joseph Juran and Edward Deming (Cole, 1979; Cole and Tachiki, 1984). Both Deming and Juran made frequent trips to Japan in the 1950s. Deming emphasized statistical quality control while Juran emphasized the advantages of good group process in getting quality improvement suggestions from employees. During the late 1950s and early 1960s, many large Japanese corporations began to take quality improvement seriously. As part of their strategy to improve product quality, they made widespread use of employee problem-solving groups called quality-control circles. The rest is well known to most Americans.

Japan managed, in a relatively short time, to progress from being a low-quality, low-cost producer to being a high-quality producer and, in some cases, a price leader. At the present time, the Japanese reputation for quality in such products as televisions and cars is unmatched in the world. When American managers looked for possible causes of the dramatic turnaround in Japanese product quality, they could not help but notice the utilization of quality circles. Unlike American workers, Japanese workers (who participated in problem-solving groups) seemed to care tremendously about the quality of their products.

Lockheed and Honeywell were among the early users of

quality circles in the United States. Lockheed adopted them in its missile manufacturing facility in the early 1970s. Honeywell also adopted them in some of its high-technology defense plants in the early to mid-1970s. Interestingly, the Lockheed program, which had an initial flurry of success, was discontinued and it was not until the 1980s that Lockheed returned to the use of quality circles. Honeywell has continued to use quality circles and has expanded their use (Kanarick and Dotlich, 1984). They have become an important part of the management style of the corporation and have led Honeywell to talk about a complete cultural change toward participative management.

Not until the late 1970s did quality-control circles become widely used in the United States (New York Stock Exchange, 1982). At that time, there were only a handful of consultants educating American managers about the advantages of quality circles and offering to install them in American businesses. One of the original consultants, Wayne Reiker, was a manager in the Lockheed plant where circles were first adopted. Despite the discontinuation of circles in his plant, he has become a widely recognized consultant on quality circles. By 1982, there were over two hundred registered quality-circle consultants, and it was clear that quality circles had become a major management tool in the United States. The 1985 national meeting of quality-circle consultants and facilitators was attended by over two thousand people and there were over sixty firms advertising their training materials.

Characteristics of Quality Circles

As with any management practice, the actual characteristics of quality circles differ from situation to situation. This is because companies adapt the basic model to their particular situation and consultants' recommendations vary regarding the way in which circles should be designed and installed. Nevertheless, there are enough similarities among the different approaches that it is possible to talk about a general quality-circle model with the major characteristics discussed below.

Membership. The membership of most quality circles is

composed of volunteers from a particular work area or department. Rarely are all the members of a work group involved.
Typically, there are more volunteers than spaces available in the
circle (frequently, about 80 percent of the people in a work
area volunteer). As a result, at least initially, some people have
to be refused the opportunity to participate. Over time, membership typically changes; in many cases, circles stop meeting and
new ones are formed in the same work area. Ultimately, in mature quality-circle programs, most individuals who want to participate do, but it may take quite a while.

Most of the early applications of quality circles were in
blue-collar, nonmanagement areas. Recently, circles have been
tried in white-collar and technical areas, so that they are now
used throughout some organizations. They still usually do not
involve managers.

Spending Authority. Most circles have no budget or ability to spend company or organizational resources. They can
study the financial implications of their recommendation and
are often expected to, but they have no budget of their own and
do not directly control any organizational resources.

Agenda for Meetings. Quality circles are always told to
focus on improving product quality. In some organizations they
are also instructed to look at issues of productivity and cost
reduction. In no case, however, are they given a broad mandate
to look at ways in which the organization could be helped to
operate more effectively and to improve the quality of work
life. This is in contrast to union-management quality-of-work-
life programs and some other participative management techniques. Overall, the agenda of most quality circles is very clearly
stated and programmed so that it is limited to just quality and
perhaps productivity discussions.

Rewards for Performance. In most quality-circle programs there are no direct financial rewards for coming up with
good ideas or cost savings. People typically are paid for participating in the meetings, since they are held on company time,
and there are often noncash recognition awards for groups that
are highly successful. To an extent, this follows the Japanese
model where pictures, awards, banquets, symbols, and so on

are given to quality circles that are particularly effective. It is amazing to see the variety of awards that companies give to their quality circles. I have seen enormous creativity go into the development of T-shirts, logos, hats, and award ceremonies. In Northrop Corporation, names have included "Tiger by the Tail" and "Team-Hornet."

Occasionally companies allow quality circles to get a cash award through their already existing suggestion programs. These typically give employees a payment based on an estimate of the savings that will result from the suggestion during the first year. In its "pure" form however, quality circles do not have a financial incentive feature and usually great stress is placed on the fact that the rewards for participating in them are intrinsic, not financial.

Training. Most quality-circle programs place a heavy emphasis on training. Particularly at the beginning, circle members are trained in group process and in problem-solving techniques. This training is often done by consultants. It does not usually include the kind of statistical quality-control methods that Edward Deming made an integral part of the Japanese quality-control circles. In the American context, the emphasis seems to be much more on group process and on problem-solving techniques, such as how to identify a problem, how to brainstorm solutions, and how to present solutions to others.

It is common for a quality-circle program to involve ten to twenty hours of training per individual and for companies to buy a prepared training package from consultants. Most consultants sell a package of training materials for quality-circle participants at a price that is determined by the number of participants. Prices of $200 per participant are common. There are a number of very well-developed multimedia packages available.

Information Shared. In most quality-circle programs there is little downward sharing of information about company operating results, costs, plans, and so forth. Quality-circle participants are asked to operate in a vacuum as far as the operating results and long-term plans of the organization are concerned.

Meeting Frequency. Quality circles typically meet on a

regular basis, often at two-week intervals. Meetings last from one to two hours. As people become involved in problem solving and in developing particular solutions they may meet longer than this. It is not uncommon for quality circles to meet on their own time in order to develop their ideas and presentations for top management. In Japan they almost always meet on the employees' time!

Leadership. Most quality circles are not led by the manager in the work area where they operate. Instead a "facilitator" is provided to meet with the groups. This person has usually been trained in group process but is not necessarily technically knowledgeable with respect to the work procedures and methods. This person's job is to help the group prepare their solutions, work effectively as a team, and, ultimately, help them present their solutions to management.

Installation Process. Quality circles are typically installed in a top-down manner. That is, someone at the top of the organization decides that quality circles are attractive and mandates that they be tried in the organization. The installation often goes immediately to the lowest level of the organization where volunteers are asked for. Many of the middle levels of the organization and the staff support people are ignored in the early phases of quality-circle installation, which is typically handled by the facilitators. After being trained by consultants, they form the groups, organize the presentations and handle the upward flow of communications.

Power. Quality circles have no formal authority in the organization except to meet and make suggestions. As such, they are not particularly threatening to the basic management prerogatives in the organization. Many consultants, such as Reiker, sell quality circles on the basis that they do *not* require a change in most top-down management styles.

An important part of every quality circle's activity is presenting its ideas to management for approval. This selling or presenting of ideas is usually carefully planned and involves several different levels in the organization. The employees usually have only their expertise and the credibility of their arguments to help them. In a few cases, however, I have seen top management order acceptance of the initial suggestions of the circles in order to get them off to "the right start."

Effects of Circles

We can now look at quality circles in terms of how they affect information, power, rewards, and knowledge. No systematic communication program associated with quality circles moves information downward in the organization. However, since circles often involve people from different areas, circle members may develop a broader understanding of the product or service, and they may come to appreciate other people's problems and perspectives. In addition, as they go through the process of developing solutions, figuring their cost, and presenting them to management, they often learn a considerable amount about the constraints and issues their organization faces. They may also learn something about costs and about the role of capital.

Quality circles facilitate the upward flow of information about ideas for improvement. This is probably their major contribution. Since circles present their ideas to higher-level managers, the program typically leads to a new type of communication that is quite important. It can have a positive impact on both management and the employees who present their suggestions. I have seen a number of top-management groups very positively impressed by quality-circle presentations. They find out that rank-and-file employees can get involved in the organization in the same way that they do. Presenting their ideas to upper management is understandably a big event for most circle members; it involves their using skills they do not usually utilize and has them meeting with high-status people.

Some knowledge building takes place in an organization as a result of the installation of quality circles. The training program usually increases people's problem-solving skills as well as their communication and interpersonal skills. As such, quality circles typically lead people to feeling more competent and to being more skilled in certain areas. However, participants do not usually learn much about particular work methods or procedures such as scheduling and inventory. Instead, they learn how to problem solve, how to interact, how to make presentations, and how to deal with others. These are important skills to learn *if* the organization plans to move to other forms of employee participation. However, they are infrequently used in quality-circle programs (once a week for an hour or two, at the most!). As a result, their development is limited and they can be as much a source of frustration as satisfaction.

Quality circles have little power to affect most decisions that are made in organizations. In fact, they represent a parallel structure to the traditional hierarchical authority. That is, *all* the traditional power relationships remain in place when quality circles are installed. The difference is that for an hour or two every week, people have the chance to meet in a special situation where there is a free exchange of ideas and thoughts about improvement. Workers also have the opportunity to present their suggestions to the traditional hierarchical structure, which usually has no mandate to accept the results of the quality circle. The quality-circle program actually has no formal authority.

The parallel structure that is created to manage a quality-circle program can be quite large in a well-established program. It often includes a program director, facilitators, and trainers who are assigned full-time to the support and management of the program. No studies detail just how many employees it takes to run a quality-circle program. My observation is that at least one full-time person is required for each six to ten circles. For example, in 1985, Northrop reported having eleven staff people and close to two thousand rank-and-file employees involved in quality circles and associated activities. Obviously, this indicates that there are significant costs associated with quality-circle programs, although I have never seen a good study of all the costs.

A subtle change in the power structure of organizations may occur when circles are used. Since knowledge and information are a kind of power, there may be some shifting of power to lower-level participants. This shift can be quite dramatic in cases where top management mandates that the circles' suggestions be taken seriously. As was mentioned earlier, in some cases top management has even ordered that all ideas be accepted in order to "encourage the groups and show them we are serious." However, most companies simply give circles their "day in court" and thus, their only power is the power of their ideas and presentation skills.

Since few quality-circle programs involve sharing financial rewards, the reward systems in most organizations go unchanged. There are, of course, some exceptions, as in programs that estimate the anticipated savings from the circle's ideas and then give the circle a share of the expected savings. One program gave everyone a savings bond for each suggestion. In the first year, over six hundred bonds were awarded, but only one suggestion was implemented. More typical are the award programs at Xerox and Honeywell. They emphasize recognition in the form of T-shirts, meetings with top management, and pictures in newspapers.

It is important to note that quality circles cover only a percentage of the work force and thus are not organization-wide in their nature. For example, even in companies like Honeywell and Westinghouse, which have used quality circles extensively, many plants and locations do not have them. Even in those locations where they exist, some departments (often engineering and office groups) do not have them. In addition, they cover only a small portion of the person's time in a workplace. They do not change the ongoing day-to-day activities of the individuals who participate.

Overall, quality-circle programs do not change organizations substantially. They do not represent a major move toward having lower-level employees psychologically or financially participating in their organizations. Particularly in the area of human resources, they leave unchanged such important systems as promotion, selection, and pay. The one thing that they change is the training system in ways that give people new skills and expertise. Their major impact is in developing suggestions and providing a vehicle for processing suggestions that come out of the problem-solving sessions. Thus, they help assure that the ideas will be heard. This is important but it is far short of the type of participation which occurs in some of the programs that will be discussed in later chapters. Because they have a limited impact on power, information, rewards, and knowledge, there is little reason to expect that quality circles will have a major impact on organizational effectiveness.

Life Cycle of Quality-Circle Programs

My research indicates that quality-circle programs have definite life cycles (Lawler and Mohrman, 1985). This life cycle needs to be understood in order to assess quality circles and to make recommendations concerning their use. The first issue that circle programs must deal with is membership. Since they are staffed with volunteers, there is always some concern on the part of management over whether there will be enough volunteers. This concern is usually quickly eliminated when the call for volunteers produces many more volunteers than can be incorporated in the circles that are planned. This is further evidence that people really want to be involved in decisions that affect their work. For decades, research has shown that people want to participate in decisions that affect their day-to-day work situation. In addition, the idea of being in a problem-solving group is much more attractive to most workers than continuing to do their regular activities, which often are boring, repetitive, and tiring.

The initial enthusiasm usually carries through the training and the initial meetings of the quality circles. In most circles, it also carries through the identification of some initial problems and the ultimate identification of solutions to several important problems. The few quality circles that fail at this stage do so because they cannot identify a reasonable problem to attack or because they find the problems untractable and unsolvable. But in my experience, this is the exception rather than the rule.

Things usually continue to go well through development of the presentation of the solution and initial meetings with members of management about implementing the suggested solutions. A major problem can develop at this point: management rejection of the ideas. There are a wide range of reasons for rejection. One is simple resistance to change due to the managers' lack of participation in the problem solving. Sometimes the groups have worked on issues that are not of concern to management. For example, I have seen groups focus on lighting the parking lot and slowing the use of paper towels in the bathrooms. In addition, sometimes the ideas cost too much or management is already planning a less expensive solution to the problem.

If the ideas are accepted, publicity often begins in the company newspaper and announcements are made about the great ideas that have come out of the quality-circle program. Projected savings of hundreds of thousands of dollars are often mentioned at this point. For example, one company I work with estimated savings of $300,000 a year from a suggestion that called for buying a new set of tools (which cost $40,000) so that the employees would not have to slow production while they searched for tools.

The next step is often an expansion of the quality-circle program; more groups are formed and trained. In many companies this is the high point of the quality-circle program. It appears that their ability to improve the company's performance hinges simply on creating more groups and letting them go to work. During this phase, success is often measured by the number of groups and the number of people involved—more is almost always better. One manager I interviewed called this the "by-the-numbers phase, in which many managers do the right things (start participation) for the wrong reason (the push from top management to have a program)." Company quality-circle newsletters often appear at this point. A recent one from Northrop, for example, reported on the number of groups meeting as well as on picnics and other social events.

I recently visited a major company that was in the expansion phase of its circle activity. The plant I visited was the one whose early successes encouraged the corporation to increase circles corporate-wide. A week after I was there, the company president was scheduled to visit in order to hear about their successes. They had a problem, however. Their groups had stopped meeting, so they were frantically looking for a member of an old group who could present their successes to the president. No one, it seems, was willing to tell the president that the groups were no longer meeting. Incidentally, this problem is not limited to this company. Susan Mohrman, Gerald Ledford, and I have often found that while top management is told and believes that a number of groups are meeting, many of the groups are nowhere to be found.

Additional important complications and problems appear during the expansion phase. First, implementation of many of the ideas suggested by the groups proves to be difficult. It often requires middle-level managers and staff support groups (such as engineering and maintenance) to implement change or to accept changes in procedures and practices that they developed and that are under their control. Not only does this mean extra work for them, it often implies that they have not done their job correctly in the past. Further, as was mentioned earlier, these groups are usually not part of the quality-circle process and may even find out about quality circles for the first time when the circles suggest some changes in their area of expertise. Not surprisingly, resistance is extremely common at this point.

For example, in one change effort, a quality circle focused on the purchase of new trucks for the organization. After months of study an extensive set of specifications were developed. They promised to save the organization hundreds of thousands of dollars by buying trucks that were both easier to maintain and more effective. There was great resistance from the purchasing agent and the industrial engineer to changing the specifications, even though top management approved the idea. It literally took months to get them to change the specifications. By the time the specifications were changed and the actual trucks were purchased, the group had long since disbanded in discouragement, convinced that management was simply engaged in a sham exercise to keep them quiet.

Unfortunately, the experience with truck purchasing is typical. It is difficult to institute change in organizations under any circumstances, but the difficulty increases when the change is spearheaded by a group that has no formal authority, that typically comes from the lower levels of the organization, and that is asking people who have "professional expertise" to change things that they have been doing for many years.

Perhaps the best way to summarize this point is to stress that quality circles are often seen as a significant threat to both the ego and the jobs of certain people in organizations. As a result, the ideas that they suggest often are not implemented. This, in turn, leads to disillusionment and anger from the quality-circle participants.

"Irrational" resistance is not the only reason why circle suggestions do not get implemented. Sometimes the suggestions simply prove to be impractical. Because of the limited information and knowledge most circle participants have, there is a real danger that they will develop ideas which look good to them but which are impractical given conditions they are not aware of. For example, groups often develop solutions that call for significant expenditures of money (such as buying new equipment) only to find out that the money is not available or that the product is being eliminated. In one case, a circle suggestion for improving quality could not be implemented because management had already bought a major piece of equipment that changed the manufacturing process. Of course, the initial success of the circle can quickly turn into disappointment and anger if the ideas are not implemented.

If quality circles get beyond the hurdle of developing and suggesting solutions that are actually implemented, the program enters a new phase. At this point, it comes up against a design feature that is basic to circles: the fact that only certain members of the organization can be involved at any point in time. Those who are not involved become upset that they are not participating. The option of rotating existing members out of quality circles while replacing them with new ones is possible, but members often do not want to leave after experiencing success. They often argue that the company should not liquidate their highly successful quality circle. I have literally seen members cry when they have to leave their circles. I have also seen circles continue for months longer than they should have, simply because people enjoy the social aspects of meeting.

If the program is expanded, it is necessary to increase the number of facilitators and to commit more and more resources to it. This ultimately leads to the phase during which most programs decline or end. Costs are high because so many groups are meeting and substantial opposition has built up among those who feel they have lost power. In addition, many of the easier problems have been solved so that the problem-solving activity does not go as well as it did with the initial groups. Finally, it usually turns out that some of the initial savings that were projected have not been realized. As one person pointed out to me, "If all the projected savings on toilet paper and towels were realized, we could have bought our own paper company by now."

The net effect of all these negative factors is usually the end of the program or a substantial reduction to the point where it is used only on a selective basis. In some cases, organizations have actually moved to less participative problem-solving programs in which management assigns the problems to groups. For example, a number of companies have moved to the Crosby (1979) approach. It is more comfortable because it is clear that management is in control and it is congruent with the management practices in most traditionally managed organizations. On the other hand, in one Honeywell facility, the move has been toward a more participative approach: self-managing teams (to be discussed later). In another Honeywell facility, quality circles are used on an as-needed basis. Typically this means that when quality problems develop because of new products or technology, circles are activated to work on the problems. Once quality has improved, the program goes into hibernation.

Long-Term Issues

Perhaps the most serious long-term problem with quality-circle programs is that they may raise expectations which cannot be filled by the typical quality-circle design. To the degree that people feel competent and powerful in their quality-circle activities, they may challenge a number of basic assumptions about the way that their organization is run. Because quality circles are a parallel structure, by design, they leave the day-to-day work activities of individuals intact. People can be, therefore, absolute geniuses in their quality circles but when on the job still be expected to do the same repetitive, boring, non-thinking task. In addition, they may be told that their idea saved the company hundreds of thousands of dollars, but they are not rewarded for this. The savings, in short, all go to the company and not to the suggestor.

In one study, Susan Mohrman, Gerald Ledford, and I found evidence that a kind of Catch-22 operates with respect to financial rewards. The success of a program depends on positive feedback. Management needs to report savings and give credit to the quality circles. This, in turn, highlights the advantages of the program for the company and raises the issue of financial payoffs for the employees. Ironically, this rarely comes up in unsuccessful efforts or where no savings are claimed—the programs simply end.

Quality circles can set up expectations and desires for broader participation in decision making and financial gains, but the structure itself does not allow these to be met. As mentioned earlier, quality-circle programs do not allow the financial gains that are realized to be shared broadly in the organization. Nor are they capable of changing the overall structure of the organization—the way jobs are designed or the way work is done.

Quality-circle programs can also change people's ideas of their own competence, and this often calls for changes in the organization's career system. Management careers often look more attractive and attainable to those who have done well in problem solving. Since many quality-circle participants are not trained in management skills, they ask for career tracks and training which will lead them into management.

In short, a quality-circle program may lead to a demand for movement toward a more participative management system. If management is prepared to change, this can be an effective way to start participative management. However, if it is not, the quality-circle program can result in the alienation and disappointment of those people who are most effective in the program—the people who come up with good solutions.

In summary, quality circles are unlikely to be sustainable over a long period. It is unlikely that the typical quality-circle program can continue in its pure form for much more than five years. By this time, it is likely to be killed, either by its initial failures to implement ideas, or, in the case of implementation, by raising people's expectations and demands for additional rewards and participation, with resultant disappointment when the organization does not meet these expectations.

Japan Versus the United States

It is interesting to compare quality circles in the United States with those in Japan. To the best of my knowledge, there is little evidence to suggest that quality circles are killed by their success in Japan. Many of the leading companies have had programs for several decades. They have recently established a new company reward to supplement the Deming prize (named after the American), which is given to the best company program. The new award goes to companies that have sustained the program for at least five years after receiving the Deming award. There is little evidence, in Japan, that quality-circle programs lead to workers' expecting additional payment or wanting to change the career system or the way jobs are designed and organizational decisions are made. In short, employees seem to be happy remaining in basically a suggestion mode with respect to members of higher management.

At first glance it may seem surprising that the situation differs in Japan, but it should not be. The American work force is clearly very different and, as a result, should be expected to respond differently to alterations in the decision-making structure. As was indicated in Chapter Two, the American work force is very favorably oriented toward participation and, therefore, is less likely to be satisfied with playing a basically consultative role in workplace decisions. Thus, it should not be surprising that a program that provides limited participation is successful in Japan but has a different result in the United States. After all, the United States is a different culture with a radically different work force. We do not have the traditional authoritarian structures and culture that exist in Japan. Democracy is, and has been for centuries, one of the most important core values in our society.

In addition to societal differences, Japanese organizations

differ in other ways that help support their quality-circle programs. For example, they have a form of gainsharing that allows employees financial participation and rewards them for their suggestions. They also have a program of lifetime employment that assures that workers will not be laid off even if they come up with labor-saving ideas. It also ties their long-term interests much more closely to those of the organization, since both parties know it is a virtually permanent working relationship.

Evaluation of Quality Circles

The literature on quality circles is devoid of comprehensive objective assessments of their impact on organizational effectiveness and the quality of work life. There are a number of reasons for this, one of which is their newness in the United States. It takes a number of years before any management innovation is systematically assessed by multiple research studies that look at its costs and benefits. In addition, many circles are supported by people who believe in them as a matter of faith and simply are not interested in evaluation. These people have made up their minds that quality circles are a good thing and do not want to see data on their effectiveness. Susan Mohrman and I learned about this when we published an article that was somewhat critical of circles (Lawler and Mohrman, 1985). We reviewed a number of strongly worded letters questioning our data base as well as features of our character. Finally, it is not simple to evaluate a major organization change such as a quality-circle program. There are often many hard-to-measure costs and benefits. (See, for example, Lawler, Nadler, and Cammann, 1980.)

The popular management press is full of stories about the "tremendous" savings produced by quality circles. For example, *Industry Week* (Pascarella, 1982) reports that at Loopco Industries, production costs have been reduced by *70 percent* as a result of a recent quality-circle project. The article also mentions payback ratios ranging from 4 to 1 to 8 to 1 on money spent to support quality-circle activities. A report from a Navy facility at

San Diego, California, claims savings of $2,050,413. Cole (1979), reporting on the original circles at Lockheed, states that at the end of 1977 there were thirty circles and that estimated savings exceeded $3 million with defects decreasing by two-thirds.

The savings from quality-circle suggestions often result from work-methods improvement, such as a new packaging method or a faster-running machine. The press is full of literally thousands of examples of better work methods and procedures suggested by employees. For example, in a bottling plant, a quality circle discovered a way to collect discarded bottle caps. This reduced a safety hazard and the caps were recycled, saving hundreds of dollars per day. In a packaging operation, another circle suggested storing precut packaging materials. This meant that the box cutter no longer had to be regularly adjusted. In the first six months, this resulted in savings of $208,000. It seems clear that the major way that quality circles can improve productivity is through the development of better work methods and better procedures.

Most reports of savings discuss only the "projected savings." This is inevitable because the ideas often have not yet been implemented; but it remains to be seen if many of the savings will actually be realized. One somewhat cynical manager said to me, "if it is like our suggestion program, the projected savings will soon exceed the national debt."

Many reports of the tremendous successes of quality circles ignore the costs entirely. In addition to training, which often costs $200 per participant, there is the meeting time, the moderately well-paid facilitator's time, and, of course, the executives' time while listening to presentations and reacting to suggestions. In short, there is typically a small training development cost and then a substantial ongoing cost that involves people's time.

Quality circles may have a positive impact on employee satisfaction, which in turn can lead to reduced absenteeism and turnover. The research suggests that, at least initially, people feel better about their work and their organization when they are in the circles (Cole and Tachiki, 1984). This, in turn, seems to lead to better attendance and less turnover for these people.

This organizational gain may, however, be offset by the impact of the circles on nonparticipants. We find that people who are not in circles often resent the fact that participants are able to spend several hours a month in "nonproductive" activities while they must continue working.

Below is a list that summarizes the possible advantages of quality circles.

- Improvements are likely in work methods and procedures.
- Organizations are more likely to attract and retain participants.
- Improvement of product or service quality is possible as a result of new methods.
- There is a possible increase in the rate of output as a result of new methods.
- Decision making is improved in a few areas due to better knowledge.
- Participants develop group process and decision-making skills.

Some areas of operating improvement are relatively unaffected by quality circles. These include staffing flexibility, amount of supervision, and grievance rate. Possible problems resulting from quality circles are summarized in the list below.

- Salary costs may increase due to new skills.
- Training costs will increase.
- Support personnel will increase to support circles.
- Expectations for organizational change may occur.
- Resistance by middle management will occur.
- Resistance by staff support groups can be a major problem.
- Expectations for personal growth and development will occur and if not fulfilled, will become a problem.
- Time may be wasted in circle meetings and in reviewing their suggestions.

It seems reasonable to conclude that, if quality circles are going to have a significant impact on organizational effectiveness and the quality of work life, it will have to be through developing new work methods.

Whether quality circles are a good investment for most organizations remains, in my opinion, unanswered because of the relative newness of quality-circle programs in most companies. It is clear that they can produce some positive results, but whether these results represent an adequate payback on the required investment is as yet unclear.

Uses of Circles

The American experience with quality circles seems to establish several things. First, American workers want to participate in problem solving to improve quality and productivity. Second, in many cases employees can come up with ideas that are potential cost-savers. Third, quality-circle programs tend to eventually self-destruct; they are usually not a viable long-term participative strategy for organizations in the United States.

Given the problems that inevitably seem to occur with quality circles, should organizations dispense with them entirely? There appears to be no simple answer to this question. Quality circles can be a starting point for a long-term move toward participative management. They can lead to other types of employee involvement by changing some of their design characteristics. For example, just by using intact work teams (instead of rotating membership) and by training supervisors as facilitators (instead of using professional facilitators), it is possible to ease the transition to more participative programs, such as self-managing teams. Unfortunately, many organizations find out only after several years of circle activity that they should have done things differently at the start. Time after time I have been called into organizations because they have reached a dead end with their quality-circle programs and they want to know what is next. If they start with an intact work group, the option of moving to teams is often a relatively obvious and easy choice.

The major advantage of using circles as a starting point is that they help train individuals for participative management. They also have the advantage of being just a small step toward participation, so, for very traditional organizations they represent a relatively nonthreatening place to start. They also can help pick off what one manager called "low-hanging fruit"; that is, they can solve some of the more obvious problems an organization faces.

It is wrong to view them as an end in themselves and as a permanent approach to participative management. Unfortunately, they seem to leave the organization in a state of incongruity that is not viable in the long run. As long as they are viewed as programs (which they are in most organizations), they are inevitably subject to elimination or curtailment.

Finally, it is worth noting that the widespread adoption of quality circles may tell us something about how American management thinks about organizational change and participation. Time after time, I have found that the two features that make them so attractive to American management is their programatic nature and the fact that they *do not* change the organization. With quality circles, it appears that management can clearly determine in advance what it is getting and can buy a certain amount of it for a fixed price. Further, they *do not* move power away from the traditional hierarchy. As a parallel organization intervention they leave the power comfortably resting in the hands of the management group that has always had power to make decisions in the organization. Thus, top management does not find them threatening and does find them comfortable to purchase as a commodity. Some consultants even argue that quality circles are not a change in management style but are simply a piece of technology to be used. As I have stressed, if this is the way they are viewed, they inevitably end up self-destructing, but in the process, they may have some positive effects on the organization.

5

Employee Survey Feedback

Attitude surveys are important management tools in many organizations. In this chapter, we are particularly interested in organizations that use them to encourage, structure, and measure the effectiveness of employee participation. It is important to acknowledge at the outset that surveys often are not used for this purpose. Rather, they are used to get a general sense of the workplace and to keep top management in touch with the attitudes, values, and reactions of the employees. IBM and Sears use them very effectively for this purpose. In short, they help in upward communications and in policy decisions. Before we discuss in detail how attitude surveys are used to aid participation, some background information is needed.

Background on the Use of Attitude Surveys

The use of attitude surveys in organizations dates back to pre–World War II. However, the extensive use of surveys by large organizations began in the 1950s and continues. Early users of surveys include General Motors, Sears, AT&T, and IBM. At first, surveys were primarily used for opinion polling. They provided management with information about how people in the organization felt about policies and practices and, in general, how satisfied they were with their jobs. (Exhibit 1 shows some sample items for those who are not familiar with attitude surveys. Also see Nadler, 1977, for an excellent discussion of surveys.) It was assumed that survey information would help guide in the establishment of human resource policies and monitor employees' attitudes.

Exhibit 1. Typical Survey Items.

Write a number in the blank for each statement, based on this scale:

How much do you agree with the statement?

1	2	3	4	5	6	7
Dis-		*Dis-*				
agree	*Dis-*	*agree*		*Agree*		*Agree*
strongly	*agree*	*slightly*	*Neutral*	*slightly*	*Agree*	*strongly*

——— 1. My opinion of myself goes up when I do this job well.
——— 2. Generally speaking, I am very satisfied with this job.
——— 3. I feel a great sense of personal satisfaction when I do this job well.
——— 4. I frequently think of quitting this job.
——— 5. I feel bad and unhappy when I discover that I have performed poorly on this job.
——— 6. I am generally satisfied with the kind of work I do in this job.

The early period of survey use was important because it helped develop the technology. It gave organizations and researchers a chance to test different questions and questionnaire formats and to become comfortable with the practice of passing out paper-and-pencil questionnaires to employees. It also taught organizations how to process and interpret survey data.

In the 1960s, relatively sophisticated methodologies for the use of attitude surveys developed. General Motors, Sears, IBM, and other companies became large-scale users of attitude surveys and developed considerable expertise in the collection, analysis, and feedback of attitude survey data. These companies established small internal corporate staff groups that provided technical support for the use of attitude surveys. These staff groups are small in most corporations (two to four people in such organizations as Weyerhaeuser, Bank of America, and Honeywell) but in a few (such as IBM), they are quite large, with as many as sixty to one hundred staff members. In addition, a number of consulting firms and university-based research organizations, such as the Institute for Social Research of the University of Michigan, developed their own surveys and sold them to the business community (see Taylor and Bowers, 1972).

By the 1970s, attitude surveys had become a very common practice in most large organizations. In fact, in many, such as IBM and Sears, they became standard operating practice. Every employee was expected to fill one out on a regular basis and to get feedback concerning the results. Literally hundreds of consulting firms offered attitude-survey consulting services. In addition, some of the large corporations that were heavy users of attitude surveys formed a users' group to share survey results. The group is called the Mayflower group and today has over thirty members, including General Electric, General Motors, Sears, Bank of America, Honeywell, Kodak, and IBM. These organizations exchange data with each other to get a collective sense of the relative frequency of different responses. This gives them a chance to determine what is a "good" answer and how their employees compare to other employees.

Today, most large corporations use attitude surveys (New York Stock Exchange, 1982). A significant percentage—probably more than half—does regular attitude surveys. Of these, a much smaller percentage uses them for participative-management purposes. The most common use of attitude surveys is still for public polling. For example, Weyerhaeuser, Honeywell, Sears, Kodak, Citicorp, Merrill Lynch, and a large number of other large corporations regularly sample their employees to gain a sense of how they feel about the corporation. They use surveys as an upward-communication device that has little effect on power, knowledge or rewards.

In many respects, attitude survey work is like taking a person's temperature. It does not tell you what the nature of the illness is, but if you know what "normal" is you can get an idea of whether the patient is in good health or not. By exchanging data, companies get a better sense of what is normal. This service is now provided by many outside consulting firms who have accumulated answers for a large number of companies. Figure 1 shows one use of these data. Hughes Aircraft data from 1981 and 1984 are compared to national norm data. Interestingly, not only did results improve from 1981 to 1984, the attitudes were more positive than the norm for other companies.

Figure 1. Attitude Survey Comparison.

Overall, how would you rate Hughes as a place to work compared with other companies in this industry you know about?

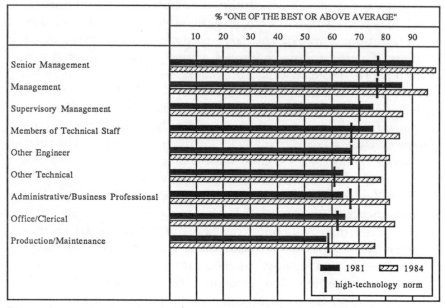

This was the most general question asked about employee attitudes toward the company. The chart above shows results for each job category. In all groups, responses were strong and positive. Here, and throughout the survey, results showed a significant improvement since 1981 and are higher than the 1984 high-tech industry norms.

Source: An internal publication of Hughes Aircraft.

In some organizations, surveys are tied into union-prevention efforts. Many companies score their attitude surveys for union propensity and take quick action when the survey results show employees to be union-prone. There is some evidence that attitudes toward pay, supervision, and overall job satisfaction are good predictors of unionization and thus they are watched quite closely.

Despite the prominence of attitude surveys in corporations and the importance attributed to them, thus far no large organization has chosen to share its data with its stockholders or the general public. One small company I worked with, Graphic Controls (see Mirvis and Lawler, 1984), actually included its attitude survey data in its annual report to give the investors and the public at large an idea about how people feel about working there. A survey of their stockholders showed that they found this information to be valuable.

People Express Airlines regularly surveys (at least semiannually) in order to monitor how its participative management approach is working. If negative data appear, the approach is changed. Ford and General Motors use surveys as part of their union-management quality-of-work-life programs (see Chapter Eight). When used in this way, surveys actually do affect power because, as in quality circles, upward communication results in change.

A few companies have highly developed participative-management programs built around survey data. IBM is probably the primary example of an organization that uses survey data for the purposes of internal problem solving and participative management. This use of surveys, which is often called "survey feedback," was pioneered by the Institute for Social Research at the University of Michigan and will be elaborated upon in the remainder of this chapter (Bowers and Franklin, 1972).

Survey Feedback and Organizational Change

The survey-feedback methodology can be traced to the 1950s and the work of such people as Rensis Likert at the University of Michigan. Survey feedback is similar to quality circles in the degree to which it moves information, power, skills, and rewards to lower levels in the organization. But before considering how much it affects these four factors, we need to briefly outline the steps that are typically taken in a survey-feedback program (see Nadler, 1977; also Bowers and Franklin, 1972).

The first issue is the selection of the data-gathering instrument. Large organizations, such as General Motors and IBM, have developed their own surveys and tend to use the same questionnaire items in all parts of their organization. They may allow for certain local questions that adapt the questionnaire to a particular location but the core of the questionnaire remains unchanged from location to location and from year to year. This allows them to tell two things: first, how the overall attitude toward any issue has changed over time, and second, how the parts of the organization compare with each other and how they have changed.

It is also possible to use one of the many commercially available questionnaires that have a core set of items as well as space for items that are of particular interest to a specific organization. In the case of the better commercial instruments (for example, those offered by International Survey Research and Opinion Research Corporation), national normative or comparative data are available. This allows organizations to get a good sense of how they compare in key attitude areas.

Almost all survey-feedback programs are based on well-developed questionnaires with at least some normative data. They also typically include some local questions that are often chosen by a committee of employees from the survey location. This group may also help plan and guide the data collection and survey-feedback process, which not only provides local input but also allows the group to develop ownership. It also helps to assure that the survey professionals are aware of local issues that might affect the questionnaire administration and interpretation. Overall, it represents the beginning of the participative process since it allows some lower-level participants to affect the survey process.

In most cases, the questionnaires are administered on company time in the workplace. Employees are given an hour or more to fill out the questionnaires. They are almost always guaranteed anonymity and great effort is made to assure that no one at the local site sees the individual questionnaires. At the time of administration, careful explanation is made of the way in which employees will receive feedback.

Some companies prefer not to take workplace time to complete questionnaires so they mail them directly to the employees' homes. Although this approach can work, it usually leads to a significantly lower response rate. In well-handled workplace administrations, it is common to get at least a 90 percent response rate, whereas, when the questionnaires are mailed out, a 50 percent to 60 percent response rate is considered good. In addition, the quality of the data may deteriorate when it is mailed to the home, since home distractions and employee playfulness (such as having the family fill it out together) may lead to lower-quality data.

Concurrently with the collection of the data, some important training activities need to take place. The extensiveness of this training varies greatly, depending on the number of times the questionnaire has been distributed in the organization and the organizational theory or model that is followed. In the most extensive model I am aware of, a week of training is done at the time of the first use of survey feedback. In this model, the entire management group spends a week in "concepts training." This training acquaints managers with the organizational theory underlying the questionnaire and in how to interpret, understand, and feed back the data to their subordinates. Often this training includes their stating an organizational ideal toward which they would like to see their organization move. This ideal is compared with the reality of the data at the time of feedback.

IBM has its own first-rate internal training program. It includes group-process training that helps managers deal with the group problem-solving discussions that are usually part of the feedback process. Some companies (such as Bank of America) neglect this training and, as a result, accomplish less.

In addition to the training that is given to the management group, more detailed training is often given to a small core group of survey feedback facilitators. These are usually not personnel people but line managers who facilitate the discussion of the survey results. This training typically involves an extra week of training. It stresses group process and decision making. In many respects, these individuals have a role in the feedback process that is similar to the facilitators' role in quality-circle programs.

Once the training has been completed and the data are analyzed, the survey feedback process can begin. Typically, it involves intact work groups meeting with their manager and a facilitator to discuss survey results. In most models the facilitator meets beforehand with the manager so that he or she is familiar with the data and is prepared to discuss them. If one of the more sophisticated survey instruments is used, comparative data are usually provided to the work groups. Thus, the work group knows how its scores compare with the responses in their organization and with other organizations. These work group meetings usually begin with a review of the work group data.

Each work group gets its average score on each item. It also typically sees the distribution of responses. Employees are encouraged to elaborate upon why they think the data turned out the way they did and, ultimately, to discuss ways that the situation could be improved so that the data would be more positive. The first meeting of the work group takes place during work hours and is often two or more hours long. At the end of the meeting, the group decides whether it needs to meet again. In successful survey development efforts, problem-solving meetings may continue for several months. The facilitators help to distinguish between issues that can be solved within the work group and those that need to be reviewed at higher levels. They then refer to top management those that need their attention. For example, most groups cannot deal with pay issues because pay plans are organization-wide, so these issues are referred upward.

The survey-feedback process typically begins with top management, which gets its own data and data for the organization as a whole. The data are then sent down the organization. The purpose of this directional flow is to give top-level management the first opportunity to digest the data. They often produce a report containing their reaction to the data that is then published in the company newspaper or is distributed in a letter.

Survey-feedback programs are usually done on an eighteen-

or twenty-four-month cycle. This amount of time between surveys seems to suit most organizations well. It allows for all the feedback meetings from the previous administration to be completed and is usually enough time for new issues to arise.

One interesting issue concerns the kind of data to which different parties in the survey program are entitled. Specifically, the issue revolves around the degree to which higher-level managers can see the data from their subordinates' work units.

In some survey programs, the manager is given data only for his or her work group and for all the people who report to it. Thus, the manager cannot tell which lower-level work units have particularly positive data and which have particularly negative data. The rationale for this is that if the manager has detailed data there will be a tendency to personally control and attempt to correct things at lower levels. It is reasoned that correcting a situation is up to the immediate supervisor and should not be based on the direct intervention of the top-level manager. Of course, if a manager wants to share the data for his or her group with the boss, there is nothing in the system to prevent it! Although this approach sounds good, in my experience, most upper-level managers find it unacceptable. It runs counter to the very reason they are doing a survey: to find out with some specificity what is going on.

The alternative is to allow supervisors to see the data for their subordinates before they are seen by higher-level managers. Ultimately, however, the data are shown to the managers. Thus, it allows higher-level managers to use survey data as a control device with respect to managers who report to them. Because they can see how different parts of the organization responded to the survey, they can, in effect, hold lower-level managers accountable for the attitudes of their subordinates. This can have a positive effect since it can allow the organization to identify particularly ineffective managers. On the negative side, however, it turns the survey away from being a self-correction device that is given to managers for their use in working with their subordinates. It becomes a control device that can be used by the upper levels of management to reward and punish lower-level managers.

Survey Feedback and Participative Management

The survey-feedback process does not represent a dramatic change in the power structure of an organization. It temporarily provides an additional amount of power to the employees. When the process goes well and numerous meetings are held to work with the survey data, it provides individuals the opportunity to at least suggest improvements to management. In this sense, it is very much like quality circles. Feedback meetings may have a little more direct influence than quality circles, however, since the immediate manager is there listening to the ideas and an intact work group is discussing them. Thus, if something comes up that affects only the work group and that the manager can implement, a feedback session can turn into a decision-making meeting. This, however, is typically at the discretion of the manager and is by no means guaranteed. Finally, since the agenda for the meeting is usually open-ended, the potential exists for the group to talk about things that cannot be discussed in most quality-circle programs (for example, supervisory behavior and pay).

There is a second way that the survey-feedback process can, to a limited degree, give power to people at the lower levels in an organization. In organizations that use the survey data to evaluate and control the behavior of managers, negative data can seriously harm the managers' careers. Thus, subordinates who fill out a questionnaire in a particularly negative fashion are exercising some power over their boss. It is primarily a veto power over the manager's future in the organization; nevertheless it is a type of power. I have seen this kind of power exercised in some companies. Subordinates have gotten together "to tell it like it is" and have ended the careers of managers. I have also seen fearful managers take action to ensure that their data would not be too negative. One manager identified the "bad attitude people" and scheduled them all for a vacation when the survey was to be administered. Another manager gave a surprise pizza party a few days before the survey administration.

The survey-feedback process gives less power to employees than do quality circles in several ways. First, lower-level employees typically are not trained in decision making and are often unsure about procedure in survey-feedback meetings. Second, the groups are only required to have one meeting, so if a manager wants to quickly terminate the feedback process, it can be done. At least with a quality circle, there is usually a commitment to multiple meetings.

The survey process dramatically increases the upward flow of information in organizations. It helps acquaint top management with the attitudes and feelings of lower-level employees. In this respect, it is one of the most effective participative-management technologies. It collects large amounts of data in a very systematic form and quickly reports them upward. Unlike quality circles, however, it does not necessarily surface ideas for improvement at higher levels.

When survey feedback is done well it also tends to improve the downward flow of information. It does this when management responds to the suggestions from the feedback session and when it communicates the survey results. In addition, when the organization shares the survey data results with the work force it gives people, often for the first time, a collective sense of how other people feel about working for the organization. This can provide additional power, since it may inform them that there is general dissatisfaction with issues that they personally have been concerned about. In this respect, it can awaken them to the potential of forming a coalition around certain issues. This may be one of the real "sleeper" effects of using the survey-feedback approach—an effect that some managers correctly fear because it can lead to concerted collective action (for example, unionization) unless corrective measures are taken.

The survey-feedback approach leads to the development of some new skills and abilities. Clearly, concepts training and especially feedback facilitator training add to managers' participative management skills and knowledge. It often proves to stimulate their further development and career mobility.

Because the survey-feedback process relies heavily on management guidance and management facilitators, it typically does little to develop skills and knowledge on the part of nonmanagement employees. Skilled facilitators may educate employees somewhat in the process of group interaction and group decision making. In addition, the discussion of potential solutions and improvements may give the employees a better knowledge of how the organization works in a number of technical areas. This kind of learning, however, is a side effect rather than an automatic benefit of a survey-feedback program.

Survey feedback typically has no effect on the reward system of an organization; however, changes may occur in the reward system as a result of the feedback process. For example, the need for changes in the fringe benefit program or the pay system may be identified. In my experience, however, this is unusual. In most cases, the reward system is not changed as a result of the feedback process.

Survey feedback typically involves all members of an organization, thereby avoiding the problem of including only a portion of the work force. However, as we noted earlier, it usually does not change the basic systems in the organization to make them more congruent with a participative-management approach. Sometimes it suggests such changes, but it does not guarantee that any features of the organization actually will be changed.

Overall, the survey-feedback approach has much the same character as quality circles, with one exception: it is identified as a short-term cyclical activity. It, too, creates a parallel organization. The feedback groups themselves, although intact work groups, are clearly meeting in a new way for a special purpose. Thus, they are temporary and often little is done to institutionalize problem solving. Instead, a temporary parallel organization is created. Because survey feedback has little effect on rewards, power, and knowledge, we must predict that it will do little to increase long-term organizational performance.

Results of Survey Feedback

Some research has been done on the effects of survey feedback. It shows that this approach has a positive but limited impact on both employee satisfaction and organizational effectiveness (Nadler, 1977). The Institute for Social Research, for example, has gone to some lengths to document the impact of their survey-feedback program (Bowers, 1973). The literature on survey feedback, unlike that for quality circles, contains few examples of big cost savings and is almost completely lacking in cost-benefit statements. Most companies that use survey feedback have not documented the impact of their work. Rather, it is taken as a matter of faith that it is a good process and the surveys are done as a matter of course.

Survey programs usually have a positive impact on employees' attitudes and feelings toward the organization. This, in turn, can affect union activity, absenteeism, and turnover. As was mentioned earlier, when employees feel better about their work situation, they are less likely to be absent, less likely to file grievances, and, of course, less likely to quit. Thus, if a survey-feedback process reveals problems and leads to their resolution, it can have a positive impact on these factors.

As was mentioned earlier, some organizations use their survey-feedback programs to anticipate and prevent union-organizing efforts. Since dissatisfaction is one of the precursors of organizing movements, such organizations as Sears, Westinghouse, and IBM gather attitude data in order to eliminate dissatisfaction that might ultimately lead to a significant union-organizing effort. Of course, simply measuring the dissatisfaction and having people express it will not by itself eliminate the dissatisfaction. Surfacing it, in fact, without dealing with it can be worse than not gathering the data at all. Significant changes must be made to eliminate the dissatisfaction. An effective survey-feedback program, however, that follows up on dissatisfaction can be integral to improving the quality of work life in an organization.

Perhaps the greatest potential productivity payoff from survey-feedback programs is in the area of improved work methods and procedures. The upward flow of communications from the survey-feedback groups creates an opportunity for employees to have their ideas and suggestions heard. In addition, the group-discussion format that is used in the survey-feedback process, often for the first time, allows employees to talk about particular problems and to share their ideas about the causes and solutions to the problems.

A strength of survey-feedback programs is the use of intact work groups and the fact that the concepts training and the feedback process involve all parts of the organization. This can effectively eliminate some of the resistance and resentment that often occurs in quality-circle programs because not everyone is involved. Also, survey-feedback programs do not create ingroups and out-groups since every group and every employee in the organization participates directly in the process.

In some important respects, survey-feedback meetings are not structured as well for work-methods improvement as are quality-circle meetings. They do not specifically target quality and productivity and participants are typically not trained in problem-solving techniques. Finally, they do not have the ongoing charter to operate that quality-circle programs have.

Perhaps the biggest weakness in the survey-feedback process is that it mainly depends on the manager of particular work groups to make things happen. Managers can simply hold one or two meetings with their work group, review the data, and call it finished. This fulfills their minimum feedback commitment to the employees as mandated by top management. If the process stops here, little is accomplished. All that is actually accomplished is a catharsis on the part of the employees and the surfacing of some issues. This can have a negative rather than a positive effect, since people may become collectively aware that there are serious problems that are not being dealt with. The recognition of these problems can stimulate even greater dissatisfaction and a greater intolerance for the fact that nothing is being done to solve them.

The positive effects that may result from an effectively run survey-feedback program are summarized below.

- Improvements in work methods and procedures may be suggested.
- Attraction and retention may improve if data are utilized.
- Staffing flexibility is not affected.
- Quality may improve as a result of suggestions.

- Output may improve as a result of suggestions.
- Staff support level is not reduced.
- Supervision is not reduced.
- Grievances may be reduced.
- Decision making may improve as a result of better communication.
- Group-process and problem-solving skills may increase, particularly in the case of managers.

The potential negative effects of the survey feedback process are summarized below. This summary assumes that the feedback process is run in a relatively effective manner.

- Salary costs are not affected.
- Training costs are substantial if full survey-feedback model is used.
- Support personnel will increase if organization runs its own program.
- Expectations for organizational change will increase if change is promised as part of survey process.
- Resistance by middle management may occur if managers are evaluated based on survey results.
- Expectations for personal growth and development may occur if survey asks about this area.
- Lost work time will occur if groups meet and survey is completed at workplace during working hours.

When compared with the advantages discussed earlier, it suggests that advantages outweigh disadvantages. However, I know of no serious cost-benefit analysis of a survey-feedback program.

It is not simple or easy to run an effective survey-feedback program. Many organizations have run poor ones and, as a result, have gotten primarily negative outcomes. For example, when I was working at the Institute for Social Research, we did a survey for a large manufacturing organization that had never done a survey before but saw itself as a very "people-oriented, good" company. As usual, management committed to a "good, open" feedback process. Everything went well until the top-management group saw the results. Basically, they did not like either the data or the way they were interpreted by the research team. As a result, they stopped all feedback and killed the problem-solving group process. The money that was spent to gather data was not just wasted, it worsened the situation. Employees became more distrustful of management and more cynical about the chances of improving the situation. Incidentally, a consulting firm today will charge $125,000 to $200,000—a significant cash investment—to start a survey-feedback program in an organization of around twenty thousand people.

More typical than the situation where top management stops the survey-feedback process is the situation where the managers do not like the feedback process and, as a result, have either poor meetings or no meetings with their subordinates. I saw this happen recently in an aerospace company. An overall feedback meeting was held but few work groups met. Some of those that met had very poor meetings that ended abruptly when the manager felt he was being criticized or his authority challenged.

Poor feedback normally occurs in traditional top-down organizations in which the culture is not supportive of lower-level involvement in problem solving. In my experience, surveys are often difficult to use effectively in just those situations where they could be of the greatest use. For example, time after time, I find that the traditional manager who does not listen to subordinates and treats them poorly cannot use the survey-feedback process well. Thus, rather than leading to improvement, it often has no effect or a negative effect because subordinates' hopes for change are raised and then not met. On the other hand, the manager who is already effective often uses the survey to further the problem-solving process and to get useful personal feedback.

In summary, much of the effectiveness of the survey-feedback process depends on the effectiveness of individual managers in dealing with their own work groups. If they fail to use the data effectively, the survey-feedback process may have little positive impact and may even have a negative one. On the other hand, if they use the data constructively and skillfully, it can be a good vehicle for beginning problem solving and for considerably improving the work culture.

With respect to organizational change, the survey-feed-back process is best viewed as one tool that can facilitate a change in management style toward participative management. In and of itself the survey-feedback process is not an effective way to make a significant movement toward participative management. It is best used as a supporting player—not as a major actor—in changing to a participatively managed organization.

Survey data that are not directly related to the group feedback process can play several important roles in participative-management programs. They can be used diagnostically to aid in choosing among different kinds of change strategies, such as work redesign or gainsharing plans. They can also be used as a mid-course correction device once other kinds of participative programs have been enacted. Survey data can be used to check on the effectiveness of local managers and to provide them with feedback on their effectiveness. Finally, as a last resort, they can be used to weed out those managers who are not particularly skillful or effective in utilizing participative management systems. Survey data have played a role in virtually every successful organizational-change effort I am aware of, so they clearly are useful even though the survey-feedback process by itself is not a particularly effective way to change organizations.

6

Job Enrichment

Enriching the work of individuals in order to improve their motivation, performance, and satisfaction is an idea that dates back to the early 1950s. At that time, a few behavioral scientists began criticizing the traditional approach to work design. They pointed out that designing specialized, standardized, and simplified work leads to jobs that are boring, repetitive, and often machine-paced. Assembly lines where an individual repeats the same simple task every few seconds are the ultimate example of traditional work design. According to its critics, this approach creates a low-quality work life for employees, poor productivity, and low-quality products and services (Argyris, 1957). For example, a classic study of auto assembly lines pointed out that many employees on the line were dissatisfied and unmotivated (Walker and Guest, 1952). Until recently no action was taken to correct the problems in the auto industry.

Individually enriching jobs became quite prominent in the late 1960s and 1970s (Hackman and Oldham, 1980). At its simplest level, job enrichment gives individuals a whole piece of work to do and holds them accountable for it. Before we discuss the principles and strategy underlying individual job enrichment, we need to spend a few more moments describing the traditional approach to job design.

82

Traditional Job Design

Based on the work of Frederick Winslow Taylor and other industrial engineers around the turn of the century, a strong case was developed for a "new" approach to job design (Taylor, 1911). It called for dividing production work into small subparts. This led to an approach to designing jobs that emphasized standard procedures for doing them, simplification of the tasks to be performed, a high degree of specialization and, where possible, machine pacing. It was reasoned that with each individual repeating a very simple task and with careful specification of the right way to do the task, both high productivity and high quality would result.

Work simplification was the dominant line of reasoning for decades in American industry. Partly because of the fame gathered by Henry Ford's first automobile assembly line, the idea of specialized, simplified, machine-paced work spread widely throughout the United States. For many organizations, the ability to produce their product on an assembly line was a mark of maturity and some pride. For many, the auto assembly line proved the advantages for this approach. Ironically, during the 1970s, when the simplification approach was challenged the auto assembly line was often cited as an example of its failure.

The simplification approach was probably valid for many decades. It was well-suited to a work force characterized by low levels of education and multiple languages as well as relatively simple manufacturing processes that required hands, not minds. It became a key competitive advantage for the United States because it allowed organizations high productivity and utilized unskilled, low-wage employees. Further, since employees were easily replaced (most jobs could be learned in a few hours) organizations were not dependent on individuals, did not have to invest a great deal in training them, and thus had power over them.

The idea of assembly-line work has been applied not only to manufacturing situations but to service industries (such as fast-food restaurants) and paperwork organizations (such as banks and insurance processing departments). In many ways it is well suited to such tasks as check processing, insurance form processing, and many other kinds of financial service work. It is now common to go into the back offices of banks and find conveyor belts moving paper in much the same way Henry Ford moved cars through his early auto assembly plants. As in auto plants, the people are doing highly repetitive, simple work, but unlike auto workers they are low-paid, probably because most of them have not yet joined unions.

Even at the high point of the American infatuation with the assembly line, less than 25 percent of the population worked on manufacturing assembly lines. However, a much higher percentage worked in jobs that were designed with an assembly-line concept and mentality in mind. Unfortunately, no accurate figures are available to indicate exactly what percentage of the jobs were and are designed in this way. A good guess, however, is that more than 50 percent still are, despite the fact that only about 4 percent of the jobs in the United States are actually on manufacturing assembly lines. Even in such high-technology industries as electronics, many of the jobs are highly repetitive. For example, most electronics manufacturing involves the mounting of small electronic parts onto a board. This work is typically done on an assembly line with each worker adding a few more components. Workers may repeat the same actions as often as every ten seconds. Because American workers are not attracted to this type of work, it is often done by recent immigrants or is exported to Mexico or the Orient.

Assembly-line work fails to provide employees with either a sense of motivation or satisfaction (Hackman and Lawler, 1971). As a result, it creates high levels of absenteeism, turnover, and poor-quality work. The work simply is not rewarding, so people tend to avoid it and to do it poorly. As a result, it requires high levels of extrinsic rewards, such as pay, to get people to perform the jobs at all and elaborate pay-incentive plans to get them to perform the jobs effectively. The popularity of so-called "piece work" (that is, paying individuals incentives for each piece of work produced) stems largely from the motivational requirements of the simplification approach to job design (Lawler, 1981). When there is no internal satisfaction from doing good work then the organization must provide some external reward, such as money, in order to induce individuals to perform. At one point, a majority of the manufacturing employees in the United States were on this kind of plan (Lawler, 1971).

The problem with the extrinsic reward strategy is that ultimately wages and benefits become very expensive. This is most apparent in such smokestack industries as steel, rubber, and autos. In some cases, individuals are paid over twenty dollars an hour (cash and benefits) for doing work that can be learned in a few days (a few hours, in some cases). They are, in effect, being compensated for their dissatisfaction with boring work. The extrinsic-reward approach also leads to a strictly monetary relationship between the individual and the organization, so that individuals will switch jobs to get higher wages and join unions to bargain more effectively for higher wages.

Ultimately, because of their complexity and their adversarial nature, most pay-incentive plans become counterproductive. In some cases, organizations end up with the disastrous combination of high pay and low productivity because the employees learn to beat the system. Given that employees spend eight hours a day doing their jobs, it is hardly surprising that they learn them so well that they are able to defeat even the most sophisticated incentive plans. The tragedy is that their intelligence and effort go into beating the system rather than into improving performance. In one tire-manufacturing situation, for example, I observed employees getting top pay for producing only a few tires a week while their incentive plan called for them to produce over a hundred per week in order to get this rate of pay. In another situation, most employees were expected to earn a 30 percent bonus, but in fact they earned an 80 percent bonus. This would have been no problem if the productivity was high, but it was not; the employees were beating the plan.

The traditional approach to job design also requires large numbers of managers and staff support people. Managers are needed for control because the work itself does not lead to self-control. Engineers, schedulers, personnel managers, and other staff support people are needed because the workers do not design the work and the pay systems, schedule the work, train the people, and so on. Designing the work and the pay systems can be particularly time-consuming since each product and machine change requires a new design.

In summary, the work-simplification approach is often associated with (1) low-quality work because individuals do not care about product quality, (2) low productivity because individuals are not motivated to be productive, and (3) high wages because individuals demand them for repetitive, boring, unsatisfying jobs. In addition, it often leads to high levels of turnover and absenteeism, and therefore overstaffing to replace absentees and people who quit. Further, despite the fact that jobs are relatively simple to learn, training costs may be high because of the high turnover rate. Finally, the social costs are high. Although largely undocumented, it is thought that the dissatisfying nature of simplified, repetitive work causes mental problems, alcohol and substance abuse, and a general alienation from society (*Work in America,* 1973).

Job Enrichment

Approaches to making individual work more interesting were first called job enlargement and later job enrichment. The best-known approach was articulated by Fredrick Herzberg (1966) in the 1960s. Later, a book by Hackman and Oldham (1980) further developed ways in which jobs can be individually enriched. An alternative approach to making work more interesting—work teams—will be discussed in the next chapter.

Herzberg's work was particularly influential at AT&T. An extensive program of job enrichment was established at AT&T during the 1960s and 1970s under the direction of Robert Ford (1969). Estimates vary, but as many as one hundred thousand jobs at AT&T, including the telephone operator's job and the service representative's job, were probably enriched. Herzberg also worked with the Cummins Engine Company and the United States Air Force on extensive job-enrichment programs. Job-enrichment programs have also been tried in the insurance industry by Prudential and Lincoln National, as well as in a number of large banks. Today, some consulting firms specialize in individual job enrichment, which continues to be an active area of organizational change.

Principles of Individual Job Enrichment

It is best to think about individual job enrichment in terms of putting tasks back together again so that one individual is responsible for a whole product or service. Many people have even commented that it is a throwback to the idea of the individual craftsperson and the one-person business. To a degree, this is an accurate but overly simplified representation of most individual job enrichment programs.

It is useful to distinguish between vertical and horizontal expansion of the individual's job. Horizontal expansion refers to assigning additional steps in the production process to an individual. In terms of an assembly line, it would mean doing not just one station, but also those that come before and those that go after it. In this way, the individual might assemble an entire product, such as a toaster, a radio, or some other small product. An early experiment at Motorola had individuals put together an entire electronic paging device that had previously been produced on an assembly line with thirty employees. Once completed, the employees put their names on it, tested it, and sent it to a customer.

Vertical expansion gives individuals responsibility for control tasks (such as scheduling work, determining work methods, and judging quality) that require decision making. The Motorola project included vertical expansion since it gave employees the right to decide on work methods and to do their own quality control. Incidentally, Motorola claimed significant gains in quality as a result of this job-enrichment project and has since become a leading proponent and practitioner of participative management.

Most theories of job enrichment stress that unless jobs are both horizontally and vertically enriched there will be little positive impact on motivation and satisfaction. The original psychological research done by Richard Hackman and myself is quite clear (Hackman and Lawler, 1971). It indicates that unless individuals experience both vertical and horizontal enrichment, they do not feel psychologically responsible for the effectiveness of their job performance. This, in turn, means that there is little internal motivation to perform effectively. The research further argues that job enrichment will be effective only if employees value such higher-order needs as achievement, competence, and personal growth. This point led to the seemingly endless debates mentioned earlier about what percentage of the work force can be motivated by enriched jobs. Motorola had an interesting way of dealing with this issue. They gave individuals the choice of whether to work on the assembly line or on individual assembly. Over time, most, but not all, chose individual assembly; those that did not said they liked to talk and to not have to concentrate on their work.

The early work Hackman did with me, as well as his later work with Oldham, argues that high motivation and satisfaction will result only when people feel they are doing meaningful work, have responsibility for the work, and get feedback about their performance. These three characteristics are influenced by five characteristics of the work itself:

1. *Autonomy:* The freedom to do the job in the way that the individual feels is best
2. *Feedback systems:* Mechanisms for letting an individual know how well the work is being performed
3. *Skill variety:* The use of a number of the individual's valued skills
4. *Task identity:* Doing a whole piece of work
5. *Task significance:* A task that accomplishes something meaningful

All five of these job-design characteristics are necessary for internal work motivation and satisfaction. It takes all of them to create a situation where individuals' skills are challenged and where individuals feel like their tasks are meaningful.

In terms of individual job design, this approach means

that individuals have to be given a whole piece of work to do, such as the production of a toaster, the maintenance of a financial account, or the processing of an insurance claim. They also have to be given some responsibility for work methods and procedures that are used to carry out the job and they need to receive feedback on how well the job was carried out.

Approaches to Designing Enriched Jobs

Advocates of individual job enrichment differ in the process that they recommend for actually enriching individuals' jobs. Some (most notably Herzberg) recommend a top-down approach in which supervisors and managers meet to redesign the work of their subordinates. For example, at AT&T the managers met for several days to redesign the work of people reporting to them. I had the opportunity to sit in on a number of these meetings and was impressed by how involved managers got in the process and how easy it was for them to come up with enriched jobs. I also often wondered whether the new designs might have been better if the employees had been involved in the redesign process. After all, employees often have good information about their jobs and about whether or not they will respond positively to enriched jobs. Because of this, it can be important to involve the job-holders in the redesign process. This can also help to overcome resistance to change among the job-holders.

At this point, it is not known whether job-holder involvement in the enrichment process is common. The largest program (at AT&T) did not involve the job-holders in the redesign process. Some other companies' programs do. The people whose jobs would be affected were involved in a job-enrichment project at Ford Motor Company in the 1960s. In this case, the employees were accounting clerks and they not only contributed to the redesign process, they also helped work out many of the implementation problems. As with quality circles or any other organizational change, which people are involved can make a critical difference in the acceptance, implementation, and institutionalization of any change. Not involving the managers of these jobs creates the risk of their resisting the enrichment and ultimately eliminating it. Not involving the job-holders, of course, creates the risk of their being opposed to it and eliminates the benefits of their knowledge about how the work should be redesigned. Thus, as with the Ford program, I usually recommend that both employees and managers be involved in the redesign process.

Job Enrichment and Participation

In terms of our criteria for a participative program, the correctly implemented job-enrichment program affects knowledge, information, and power. All of these are increased at the lower levels in an organization. Power increases because individuals now have authority to make decisions that they previously did not have. They can now decide on certain work methods, scheduling issues, and quality standards. Knowledge is affected because with broader responsibility, individuals need more skills. In many cases, the new skills are "doing" skills (that is, how to do more steps in the production process), but they may also develop thinking skills because they need to plan work, schedule work, and decide on work methods.

Finally, the amount of information that individuals have is also likely to increase because of better feedback about how effectively tasks in their immediate work area are performed. Nothing, however, in individual job-enrichment programs leads to individuals having better knowledge of the overall operating results of the organization. Also, nothing allows them to influence issues of overall organizational policy, strategy, or design.

Typically, job-enrichment programs are installed in only a small part of an organization. That is, a few jobs or one particular type of job is identified for enrichment. Thus, only a small percentage of the organization is usually affected by the typical job-enrichment project. Even at AT&T, where perhaps a hundred thousand jobs were enriched, many more than that were left alone. The typical telephone operator still handles a call every few seconds in a standardized machine-paced manner. Over time, the jobs have become even less enriched. In their efforts to completely automate the work, the engineers at Bell Laboratories have given more and more of it to computers. (They never thought of job enrichment as a solution.) Ultimately, this may benefit the company if operators can be entirely eliminated. For the time being however, it has made these jobs yet more simplified and repetitive.

Job enrichment does not necessarily involve changing multiple systems within the organization. That is, most job-enrichment projects focus only on changing the content of the job itself and do little to change the management information system and training programs. In fact, all the other systems in the organization, including the pay and selection systems, the overall organization structure, and the nature of the supervision are usually ignored.

In this respect, job enrichment is similar to quality circles. It is different in that it does not create a parallel system, but instead changes elements of the existing organization. As such, it is likely to have some significant positive impacts. However, without other changes to support it, its durability is questionable.

Results of Job-Enrichment Programs

The literature is full of reports of successful job-enrichment programs. Recent reviews of the literature found reports of thirty job-enrichment experiments (Kopelman, 1985; Locke and others, 1980). Typical reports talk about how the work of twenty-five or so employees was both vertically and horizontally enriched and go on to specify particular cost improvements.

A good example is Northwestern Mutual Insurance. A consulting firm (Roy Walters) helped redesign work for about five hundred people who process new insurance policies. Before the change, the processing involved forty steps and was scattered across many people and floors in a building. After job enrichment, people worked in sections that served geographic regions. One person did all new-policy services and worked directly with field agents. The result was better customer service and a decrease in processing backlog.

Usually, individual job enrichment has a greater impact on quality than on productivity (Lawler, 1969). Reports of errors dropping anywhere from 10 percent to 60 percent are common. One review of twenty-one cases cites an average gain in quality of 28 percent (Kopelman, 1985). This reduction in errors and improvement in quality seems to have at least two causes. First, when individuals feel responsible for their tasks, they seem to be much more motivated to turn out a high-quality product than they were before. Second, as they gain a broader perspective on the entire product or service, they can often catch errors that might have gone undetected due to lack of knowledge. In short, they get a broader perspective on the work and, as a result, can do it better.

The effect of broader perspective was very obvious in the project done at Ford. After enrichment, the accounting clerks were often able to identify and solve problems because they understood the entire production process. Before enrichment, they simply did their part of the work and passed it on. Ironically, the work was originally specialized to prevent errors. The view was that if everyone was an expert in what they were doing, there would be less chance for an error. As is often the case, there was a single incident (the overpayment of a local hardware store for some bolts) years earlier that led to the specialization approach.

There is also evidence that enrichment can produce lower rates of absenteeism (the Kopelman review cites a decrease of 14.5 percent) and turnover and also can improve job satisfaction. Apparently, working on an enriched job is, as predicted, a more satisfying and psychologically rewarding experience; as a result, individuals are less likely to be absent and to suffer psychological problems.

Most studies make no mention of job enrichment directly producing improvements in work methods or procedures. Interestingly, the research suggests that there is no consistent positive effect on productivity. One review estimates an average increase of 6.4 percent but notes that in over one-third of the cases, there was no effect (Kopelman, 1985).

Productivity improvement does not always occur for two

reasons. First, sometimes there is an efficiency loss when individuals take on horizontally enriched tasks. Learning the skills can take time and in some cases the individual who does something only a few times a day may not be as good at it as someone who does it repeatedly. This was demonstrated in a project involving a medical products manufacturer who produced a small simple product that required employees to have good manual skills. In order to keep these manual skills at their highest levels, employees needed to use them almost constantly. Adding other tasks to their jobs reduced their productivity because it caused them to lose their rhythm. The same thing is true for other tasks that require finely tuned manual skills. For example, individuals who peel hard-boiled eggs and stuff pimentos into olives do the kind of work that is hard to enrich without a loss of productivity.

In the case of larger products, enrichment can also cause material-handling problems. With an individual assembling the whole product, it is often difficult to efficiently get the necessary parts and supplies to the individual and then to efficiently remove the completed product. We found just this problem in a study of automobile transmission assembly lines. The parts were too big to get all of them to an individual easily. As we shall see in the next chapter, this is one of the reasons most work redesign in the auto industry has used teams.

Ironically, in the transmission-assembly situation we found a way to handle the materials but another problem stopped implementation of the program. The line had a quality problem with the tightening of several bolts. As a short-term solution, the job was being done twice by different people to be sure it was done correctly. It seems one person could not be counted on to do it correctly even though it was a very simple task. While I was studying how to enrich the jobs, the engineers were designing and buying a half-million-dollar piece of equipment to solve the problem. It was installed (after all that expense it had to be) and it worked, but it left a large number of individuals on the line with repetitive jobs.

There also seems to be a motivational issue concerning productivity. As mentioned earlier, people get their sense of psychological success and satisfaction from doing high-quality work rather than from performing at a higher rate of productivity. Thus, to some degree, the lack of increase in productivity may be due as much to lack of motivation as it is to the potential inefficiencies and training complications of adding more tasks to a job.

Occasionally mentioned in the literature on enrichment are productivity gains produced by the need for fewer support services and by the reduction in managerial overhead. Occasionally, fewer maintenance services are needed, for example, because some individuals do their own machine maintenance and setup. Also, less management may be needed because some of the decisions that were made by managers are now moved to lower levels in the organization.

Despite the potential for reducing management and support services, this rarely happens. For example, even though AT&T enriched thousands of jobs, they never eliminated any levels of management until recently. Deregulation apparently has done what job enrichment could not; we increasingly hear reports of AT&T and its former operating companies eliminating levels of management. This is partly because the focus in most job-enrichment projects is not on organizational redesign but on enriching individuals' jobs. In summary, although the possibility exists, there is little evidence that individual job enrichment has regularly led to savings in overhead or indirect labor.

The list below summarizes the positive effects of job enrichment. Areas that do not seem to be affected by job-enrichment programs are staff support level, supervision level, and grievances.

- Some improvement is possible in work methods and procedures.
- A gain is likely in attracting and retaining workers.
- Staffing flexibility should increase.
- Service and product quality usually improves.
- A small increase in the rate of output may occur.
- Decision making may improve because of better knowledge.

Where Job Enrichment Is Applicable

Certain conditions must be present in order for job enrichment to be successful. These can be broken down into two broad categories: the nature of the individuals and the nature of the technology used to perform tasks.

Obviously, for job enrichment to succeed, the individuals must be capable of adding to their skills and abilities and be motivated by such intrinsic rewards as a sense of accomplishment, achievement, and competence. In the absence of the ability to learn and develop skills, enriched jobs can overwhelm the individual. Poor performance will result from a job requiring more skills than the individual possesses. For individual job enrichment to produce greater motivation and satisfaction, individuals must desire a sense of accomplishment and competence in their work. When they do, they will be both more motivated and satisfied. It is important, when applying a job-enrichment program, to assess the individuals whose work is going to be enriched and to determine if they have the right need structure and the necessary potential to develop the skills that the new job will require.

Technological constraints may make individual job enrichment inappropriate in many situations, such as if the product is simply too large or complex for any individual to produce. When there are too many large pieces that need to be put in place, one individual is often not able to master all the skills or efficiently use the skills to build the product.

Another constraint occurs when a production technology needs many people to operate it. This is true in the so-called process technologies, which are used to produce paper, oil, chemicals, and food. Individuals cannot follow a product from beginning to end. Production occurs in highly automated factories in which people are needed to monitor the flow of the product throughout the factory. Similarly, in many service organizations one individual cannot deliver an entire financial service. The technology simply requires people to be working simultaneously at different points in the process. Such technologies lend themselves more to group work designs than to job enrichment programs and will be discussed in Chapter Seven.

Limitations of Job Enrichment

Most of the problems associated with job enrichment stem from the fact that organizations are complex connected systems. Changing any one part of the system can have dramatic impacts on other systems in the organization. When work design is changed, other systems in the organization will be strongly impacted. For example, the design of lower-level employees' jobs directly affects the nature of the supervisor's job as well as the jobs of many support people. In addition, as the demands on an individual whose job is enriched change, changes may be necessary in training programs, selection programs, and pay programs.

I have seen a number of situations where, after working on an enriched job for a while, individuals demand higher pay because they do more. I have also seen them ask for bonuses or profit sharing because of the savings which have resulted. Ironically, the more organizations talk about the gains, the more employees feel that they deserve a share of the gains. This suggests that organizations should not talk about gains, but failure to do this violates the principal of giving feedback!

Finally, after individuals work for a while on an enriched job, they may come to see themselves differently and to expect much more from the organization. It is not uncommon, for example, to find individuals who, after mastering an enriched job, raise the obvious question of "what's next?" They seek new career tracks, additional tasks, and additional training. All of this calls for significant changes in an organization.

All too often organizations are not prepared to deal with the multitude of organization-wide issues that are raised by job-enrichment programs. For example, they are not prepared to change their pay system and other systems to fit better with individually enriched jobs. As previously mentioned, the net effect of this is to ultimately cancel out the enrichment activities and to upset people whose jobs were enriched because they feel the organization has not responded to the expectations it created and to the commitments it made.

Supervisors are often quite threatened by their new relationship with their subordinates and sometimes behave in ways that take away the autonomy and freedom that the enrichment program was designed to give to their subordinates. To a substantial degree, they feel threatened with the loss of their own jobs because their tasks have been transferred down in the organization while nothing has been done to enrich their jobs. Ultimately, they may resist job enrichment and systematically de-enrich their subordinates' jobs in order to protect and maintain their own work and power.

Because of the many forces that exist in organizations to de-enrich jobs, it is not surprising to come back to an organization that once had a job-enrichment program to find that the jobs are no longer enriched. Over time, the supervisors have reorganized the work to remove many of the enrichment characteristics.

This happened in an early job-enrichment project that I was involved in. The jobs of telephone operators were enriched. In order to provide vertical enrichment, some decisions that had been made by supervisors were given to operators (such as what to do with emergency calls and requests for special services). The project showed initial gains but a year later most of the gains were gone. An examination revealed that the jobs had been de-enriched by the supervisors who were now supervising so closely that their subordinates experienced little autonomy. We concluded that without removing a level of supervision, job enrichment would always be a temporary phenomenon in this organization.

Ironically, several years later, I had the chance to interview the president of AT&T. I asked him about the success of the corporation's job-enrichment effort. He rated it highly but noted that its success was limited by the structure of AT&T. When I asked what structural changes were needed, he immediately said, "fewer levels of management." To the obvious next question, "why don't you eliminate some levels?" he gave a look which said it simply was too big and politically sensitive an issue to take on. Ten years later, deregulation made it not just possible but necessary for his successor to take on this issue!

Below is a summary of the problems with job enrichment.

- Salary costs may go up
- Training costs go up.
- Support personnel can increase if staff is developed to implement job enrichment.
- Unmet expectations for organizational change can be an important problem.
- Resistance by middle management may become a problem if their issues are not dealt with.
- Resistance by staff support groups can occur if their jobs are affected.
- Unmet expectations for further personal growth and development can be an important issue.
- Conflict between participants and nonparticipants can be a problem because not all jobs are changed.

Durability of Job Enrichment

The organizational issues that come into play when jobs are enriched can ultimately mean the end of a job-enrichment effort. In many respects, the typical job-enrichment program has built into it the seeds of its own destruction. Like quality circles, job enrichment deals with a relatively small percentage of people in the organization and with just one aspect of the organization. Unlike quality circles, it does not create a parallel structure; instead it makes a fundamental change in the way work is done in the organization. In this respect, it creates a more dramatic and powerful change. It is not surprising, therefore, that it can significantly affect the motivation and behavior of the people whose jobs are enriched. At the same time, however, as with quality circles, if nothing is done to change the other systems in an organization, job enrichment is likely to eventually die.

Specifically, it is very likely to be opposed by supervisors and by support people unless something is done to alter the fundamental organizational structure and unless it is advantageous to them as well as to the individuals whose jobs are being enriched. The point was clearly stated to me by a Chrysler plant manager. He had been part of a corporate task force to study job enrichment. He and the task force concluded that it was much needed in the auto industry and ought to start with the *plant manager's job*. He correctly noted that he had little autonomy and that until his job was improved he could hardly be expected to push decisions downward.

In many respects, the counterforces to job enrichment can be much stronger than the counterforces to quality circles. This is due to the parallel-structure nature of quality circles in comparison to the core change involved when changing the work itself. Quality circles can be easily encapsulated and ignored by traditional organizations. This, of course, also makes it relatively easy to eliminate them when it is no longer politically "in" to have them. In the case of job enrichment, however, change is made in a highly visible, important feature that affects the day-to-day work activities of others. As such, it can build up tremendous opposition and strong proponents of its elimination.

Uses of Job Enrichment

Two long-term strategies are possible with respect to job enrichment. One is to simply keep enriching and re-enriching jobs. This approach has been taken by a large insurance company that has a group working full-time on job enrichment. When I interviewed them they claimed to have enriched over three thousand jobs a year for over five years. When I asked if they were not afraid of running out of jobs they said "no," because they found there was a continuing need to re-enrich jobs. This approach establishes job enrichment as a program that needs a staff and that has to be maintained and budgeted for. As such, it is always subject to cancellation, as the AT&T program ultimately was. One AT&T manager spoke quite realistically about the fate of most programs. "Programs like job enrichment come and go around here as do the people who support them. I want to stay so I don't get associated with them."

A second approach is to view individual job enrichment

as just one part of an overall change effort—a way of life. In this approach, changes are made so that other features of an organization are congruent with enriched jobs. Job enrichment is not viewed as a stand-alone participative vehicle. It is combined with other changes so that it can be institutionalized.

My bias is clearly toward using job enrichment as part of an overall change program. When used in this way it can yield long-term improvements in productivity that result from having a more motivated, knowledgeable, and empowered work force. However, using job enrichment as part of an overall change program is not simple. Two key issues need to be dealt with. The first concerns timing, or when to change the work design. As we will see in Chapter Twelve, there are few easy answers to questions concerning the sequence in which the major features of an organization should be changed. The second issue concerns whether individual job enrichment or teams represent the best approach to job design for a particular organization. As we will see in Chapter Seven, this question is somewhat easier to answer.

7

Work Teams

Designing work for teams is increasingly popular. General Motors is using teams to assemble cars; in fact, the entire design for the manufacture of their new Saturn car is based on teams. (This represents a billion-dollar bet that teams of U.S. employees can compete with the Japanese in small car manufacturing.) Volvo has built an entire auto plant at Kalmar, Sweden, around work teams. Butler Manufacturing has work teams successfully assembling grain elevators.

Giving groups tasks does not necessarily imply a movement toward participative management and a team-based approach, but in many cases it does. Typically, specific design steps are taken that give individual employees considerable responsibility for how the group operates and functions; the result is the creation of a team that takes on many management functions. (See Cummings, 1978.) Before we discuss work designed for teams and its results, let us briefly review its history.

Background on Work Teams

The history of work teams has a decidedly European flavor. Early writings are dominated by reports of a British coal mine. It was made famous by writings of Eric Trist and others interested in the sociotechnical theory of work design (Trist and Bamforth, 1951). They reported on a case in the British coal industry where workers had spontaneously created their own work team at the face of a coal mine. Team members helped each other out and even traded jobs. The researchers found higher productivity and job satisfaction in this team than in a more traditionally organized work situation with individual responsibility and accountability for specialized and standardized tasks.

The coal mine research proved to have quite an impact, particularly in Scandinavia, where, under the intellectual stimulation and guidance of Einar Thorsrud, numerous experiments were tried. Work teams were called autonomous work groups, self-managing work groups, or semiautonomous work groups. This terminology was meant to imply that not only did the work teams have responsibility for a significant area of the workplace but that they could make a number of decisions concerning when and how the work would be done. For the purposes of this book, I will refer to them as work teams.

The General Electric Company was one of the early extensive experimenters with work teams in the United States. During the 1960s, for example, they created over a hundred teams in their factories. In many cases, these work teams produced positive results but a follow-up study years later found that they tended to fade from existence over time.

The real popularity of work teams in the United States, however, did not occur until the 1970s. Spurred by the reported success of some new plants, particularly those started by Procter & Gamble and General Foods, a number of companies began to experiment with work teams. Today Cummins Engine, General Motors, TRW, Digital Equipment Corporation (DEC), Shell Oil, Honeywell, and a host of other U.S. firms use work teams in their manufacturing plants. These teams are at least partially self-managing in that they control important parts of their work process.

Much of the work team experimentation in the United States has taken place in new facilities or with new products. This aspect of work team experimentation will be discussed in detail in Chapter Ten. In the present chapter, the focus will be on work teams that are put into an existing facility or situation.

Characteristics of Work Teams

As with any participative-management innovation, the actual characteristics of work teams differ from situation to situation. Nevertheless, the following characteristics are common to most United States installations of work teams:

Membership. Membership in work teams typically includes all of the employees working in the affected areas. There is a strong belief that individuals should not be given the option of being in a work team. It is argued that if individual employees do not participate in the work team the team concept is destroyed for everyone else.

This is in noticeable contrast to job enrichment, which can be installed on a choice basis, as in the case of Motorola mentioned in the previous chapter. Often, when teams are first begun, volunteer work areas are asked for; usually, teams are started only in those areas where there is substantial interest in them. Once a work area is targeted for teams, however, membership in the team is compulsory.

Work Area Coverage. Many of the principles that were applicable to individual job enrichment are also applicable to the design of work teams (Hackman and Oldham, 1980). As previously mentioned, it is important to give people a sense of responsibility for building a whole product or offering a complete service. This principle is used for work teams as well. Each team is given responsibility for enough of a product or service so that there is a clear input and clear output for which they can be held responsible.

In the car assembly at Volvo, one work team is responsible for putting in the entire electrical system while another is responsible for doing all the upholstery work. In the Shell chemical plant at Sarnia, Ontario, a work team is responsible for running the entire plant. In the Cummins Engine plant, in Jamestown, New York, one work team is responsible for machining and completing the work on an entire piston, while another team assembles the entire engine. In short, an effort is made to build into the responsibilities of a work team the same kind of task identity, task significance, and multiplicity of skills that is built into individually enriched jobs. The difference with team design is that the responsibility for doing the work is shared among people rather than given to an individual.

In order to increase the sense of shared responsibility, as well as to accomplish a number of other objectives, members of a work team are typically "cross-trained" so that they can do most, if not all, of the tasks that fall within their work team's area of responsibility. Typically, members rotate among tasks so that each individual knows how to do all the tasks that fall within the domain of the team. This not only gives the work group flexibility in assigning members, it also gives people the same sense of ownership and responsibility for the final product that comes about through individual job enrichment, where one person actually takes the product from beginning to end.

Training. Training is very important in the establishment of work teams. Two kinds are dominant. First, there is the extensive task training which is necessary so that individuals can effectively perform multiple functions. This training may go on for years and, in many cases, is done by team members. For example, in the Shell Sarnia plant it may take as long as nine or ten years for employees to learn all the tasks that fall within the responsibility of the teams. In most situations, however, learning time is closer to three years.

Interpersonal skill training is the second important type of training for work teams. Work teams spend a considerable amount of their time in meetings and, as a result, need to be skilled not only in technical matters but in interpersonal matters. To a very significant extent, a work team is only as effective as its group process. Many people come to the workplace without the kind of interpersonal skills that it takes to make decisions, give feedback, and interact with each other in a positive manner. Thus, extensive training is often needed in order for the groups to interact effectively.

The amount of training that is needed, of course, varies

with the types of decisions that are given to the work teams, but in all cases a significant amount of interpersonal training is needed. Team members in a number of plants have often remarked to me that this training is the hardest part of being in a team. In many respects, this is not surprising since it calls for changing lifelong patterns of behavior. As will be discussed later, when poor group process occurs teams tend to be ineffective, particularly in making critical decisions regarding work assignments, peer evaluation, and pay actions.

Meetings. Work teams meet often. Usually there is one regularly scheduled meeting a week and additional as-needed meetings. The regular meeting typically deals with such things as work assignments and the regular business of the team. As-needed meetings typically deal with production problems and day-to-day work-assignment issues. In most plants I have worked with, a team can decide to stop production and hold a meeting if there are significant quality problems.

Supervision. The kind of supervision in work teams varies (Schlesinger, 1982). In some organizations, a leader is allowed to emerge and is voted on by the members of the work team. More frequently, however, a team leader is appointed and, in some cases, has responsibilities for more than one team. It is up to the team leader to see that the group process is effective and that the work is, in fact, getting done through the group process. Particularly at the beginning, this is an extremely critical and difficult role. At this time, teams are not able to make many of the necessary critical decisions and, as a result, the team leader has to be extremely active in the decision-making process. As teams mature and develop, the leader's role changes. It becomes more that of facilitator and communication link. It is often apparent at this point that team leaders can work with multiple teams.

Reward Systems. Sometimes the basic pay system in the organization changes when a work team is started. The most common change involves the installation of skill-based pay. In this pay system, individuals are paid for the number of tasks that they can perform rather than for the job they are doing at the moment (Lawler and Ledford, 1985). The tie-in between this and the cross-training that was mentioned earlier should be obvious. It is an incentive that encourages people to learn multiple tasks because it increases their pay as their flexibility and skills develop. This approach to pay helps to set a climate of personal growth and development in the work team.

Sometimes small-group or gainsharing-type bonus plans are installed in combination with work teams. Most organizations that install teams have to deal with the issue of rewarding performance sooner or later. Since the focus is on team production, it makes more sense to reward the team's or the whole organization's production than to reward an individual's performance. This is just the reverse of job enrichment programs. Interestingly, the use of group incentive plans in conjunction with work teams seems to be more common in Europe than in the United States. If anything is done with pay in the United States, it tends to be a plant-wide bonus plan rather than a small-group or team-based bonus plan.

Decision-Making Responsibility. The principles of work-team design call for important decisions to be made by the teams. The qualifier is usually added that management retains the right to challenge the teams' decisions. There is actually considerable variability in the kinds of decisions that teams can make. The observant reader may have guessed this from the multiple names that are used for work teams. Originally, they were often called "self-managing work groups" or "autonomous work groups." These names have come under increasing criticism and are used less frequently because they imply more freedom to make decisions than most teams actually have. They are also controversial because they infer that management has no power over the group and may not even be needed any more. It is common now to hear such terms as "semiautonomous work groups," "self-regulating work groups," and simply "work teams."

The key issue, of course, concerns which decisions teams will make. In highly autonomous work groups, teams make virtually all the decisions that are required to run a small business. They hire, fire, determine pay rates, determine quality, specify work methods, manage inventory, and so on. In a Cummins Engine plant the sense of a small business is reinforced by the accounting system that calculates and provides the work teams with cost data for their operation.

In less autonomous work teams, many of the human resource decisions, such as pay and selection, remain with management, but the work teams still deal with issues of setting production goals, managing their own quality, and determining work methods. This approach has been used by Olivetti in their Italian manufacturing plants for over a decade. In all cases, the teams receive direct feedback about their performance and are responsible for monitoring their performance against various standards. In most cases, they also have budgets, at least for small expenditures and have the right to recommend purchases and changes to management for large expenditures.

Installation Process. Typically, self-managing work groups are installed in existing facilities on an "experimental basis." Like quality circles, a few are tried to see how effective this idea is likely to be in a given work situation. The installation is generally done in a relatively top-down manner; that is, top management decides to try a few of them and volunteer work areas are solicited. Once several have been identified, the installation proceeds, usually with limited input from the people in the work area. At the beginning, in particular, work-team members are very much in the mode of learning and trying to absorb the idea of work teams.

In contrast to the installation of teams in existing facilities is the plant-wide installation of work teams in new plants, where there is no experimental period to see how they will work. In both cases, however, it takes a considerable period of time to develop effective self-managing teams: a good estimate is two to three years. During this time, the group is learning to deal with difficult group-process and decision-making problems and becomes more self-regulatory.

Size. There is no magical "correct" size for a work team. However, much of the literature on work teams suggests that somewhere between seven and fifteen members is optimal. Most teams are within this size range; however, teams as large as thirty exist.

There are numerous problems with very large teams, including the difficulty of developing group process with such a large group, as well as a number of problems in the work design. It is often hard for somebody to understand and see a complete work process in which thirty people are involved and, of course, it is difficult for individuals to learn and rotate through as many as thirty tasks. There is also a considerable amount of literature that suggests that group cohesiveness is closely related to group size. Too large a group tends to lead to relatively low cohesiveness. For groups to be effective in decision making and self-control they must be cohesive.

Work Teams and Participation

Work teams perform very much like individual job enrichment in terms of the effect they have on the organization—they move power to lower levels in the organization. In fact, depending on how autonomous they are, they may move considerable power to the lowest level of the organization. If, for example, they move decisions regarding pay, selection, production, and purchasing into a work team, they affect power more than individual job enrichment. All important business decisions that affect a work area can be given to the employees in that work area. For example, in the TRW plant in Lawrence, Kansas (Fortune Magazine Editors, 1982), employees have greater control than they would with job enrichment. Teams are able to deal with issues that cannot be handled by individuals, such as deciding who works on which shift, training each other, and purchasing equipment which will be used by several individuals.

The work team approach also makes a considerable impact on the knowledge that employees have. Now, instead of simply knowing one task, they are expected to learn multiple tasks. An effort is also made to move vertical tasks into the work team so the employees may learn important managerial and staff support skills. For example, in some plants, purchasing, scheduling, inventory control, and other vertical skills are made the responsibility of the team. As a result, people in the team acquire this type of knowledge.

The work team approach also creates the potential for moving considerable information to the lower levels. If the teams take responsibility for vertical skills such as scheduling and purchasing, then information about costs, business operations, and so forth, which were not previously available to lower-level participants, will be.

Reward-system changes are sometimes made in conjunction with the installation of work teams. As noted, skill-based pay is often added to encourage individuals to learn necessary skills. However, the installation of work teams may not lead to bonuses or pay rewards being tied to team performance. This may be a serious omission since it means that the financial interests of the organization and the individuals are not the same. The individuals may be more interested in learning new skills because they are rewarded for it, while the organization is interested in performance.

Overall, work teams make an important difference in the participative structure of organizations. Individuals end up with knowledge and skills, information, rewards, and power that they do not have in traditional organizations. Thus, work teams are likely to have an important positive impact on organizational effectiveness.

As was noted earlier, work teams are often established on a trial basis of one or two per location. This trial, however, may not result in the addition of more groups. As a result, work teams may involve only a small percentage of the total work force. Even where there is widespread use of teams, they are rarely used throughout the entire organization. Most technologies do not require that work teams be instituted throughout the organization. Thus, the typical organization has only a part of the work force in teams. Office and support people in plants, for example, are usually not in teams.

As was mentioned previously, some other systems are often changed when work teams are started. Most prominent among these are the training system and the pay system. Often, however, the selection system, the information system, and a host of other important systems are not changed because work teams are put in place. If work teams are installed but important interrelated systems are not changed, it is difficult for the teams to reach maximum effectiveness.

Results of Work Teams

The results of work teams are very similar to those of individual job enrichment. There are numerous substantial successes, but these do not always lead to the establishment of other teams nor even to the continuation of those that have been created (see Cummings, 1978; Hackman and Oldham, 1980; Cummings and Molloy, 1977). But before getting into the issue of dissemination and institutionalization, we need to briefly review the kind of positive results that typically come from work teams.

The areas where effective teams can provide improvement are listed below.

- Improvement is likely in work methods and procedures.
- A gain is likely in attraction and retention.
- Staffing flexibility increases.
- Service and product quality usually increase.
- Rate of output may improve.
- Staff support level can be reduced.
- Supervision can be reduced.
- Decision making is likely to improve.

There is little evidence of the consequences of work teams on grievances.

Like individual job enrichment, the creation of teams seems to produce a high concern for quality. One review found that six of seven studies reported improved quality (Cummings and Molloy, 1977). The psychological phenomenon here seems to be similar to that with individual job enrichment. When people are accountable and responsible for the production of a product, they want it to be of good quality. The team situation also provides individuals the chance to solve problems concerning quality issues and this often leads to good ideas about how to improve it.

There can also be an improvement in production because teams set production goals and get feedback about how well they achieve these goals. Production also increases because of the flexibility of the individuals. Cross-training allows them to help each other out and sometimes fewer people are needed to keep a production area operating. Groups often decide they can do their own setup, thereby eliminating the need for a setup person. I have also seen two employees run three machines, whereas previously they had insisted that it took one person for each machine.

When groups are cohesive, social pressure can play an important role in motivating performance. Valued social rewards (praise and acceptance) become dependent on group members performing well. Similarly, punishments are sometimes administered when individuals do not perform well. I have seen groups counsel poorly performing members to leave the organization; in some cases, they have actually fired them. This is in noticeable contrast to the situation in traditional plants. There I have seen good performers rejected, criticized, and even harmed because they produced too much, thereby potentially raising the standards for everyone.

One review shows that fourteen out of fifteen studies found that teams led to improved productivity (Cummings and Molloy, 1977). As groups become cohesive, membership in them becomes a very important feature of the workplace. Members are hesitant to be absent and to quit because they value group membership. For example, in self-managing work groups, it is common to find turnover and absence rates of 1 or 2 percent a year. This is, of course, much lower than the typical rates for American industry in both categories. A Volvo executive told me that a major reason his company started using work teams is absenteeism. For a number of reasons (including the government's paying workers who do not show up for work), Volvo found itself with very high absentee rates in the early 1970s. On some days rates were reportedly higher than 35 percent. Although there is no definitive research, there are reports that Kalmar (the team-based plant) has lower absenteeism.

Not surprisingly, the members of effective work teams

tend to report very high satisfaction. The group setting meets the individual's needs for social interaction and belonging. When groups are effective, they also meet needs for competence, achievement, and recognition. Finally, when skill-based pay and production bonuses are offered, individuals are also reasonably well-paid so that their financial needs are met.

In summary, the work team design creates a very satisfying and rewarding work environment that, in turn, leads to individual behavior that tends to increase productivity and reduce costs. Expensive absenteeism and turnover are reduced. In addition, because of cross-training, even if individuals are absent or leave, someone who knows the task is available to fill in. Finally, because of cross-training, the work force is extremely flexible and can double or triple up if some aspect of production needs extra help. This can be crucial when the work situation is characterized by bottlenecks or a crisis demand for individuals at one point in the process.

Work teams can also have a significant impact on the need for supervisory personnel and staff groups. If, as mentioned earlier, many vertical tasks are assigned to the work team, there can be a significant savings in overhead. Work teams can do work in areas of inventory, scheduling, quality assurance, and even middle- and upper-level management. When this occurs, significant productivity gains can be achieved by leaner staffing. These can in turn offset the somewhat higher compensation costs that are created by the skill-based pay system.

In plants where the work team concept permeates the organization, there are clearly fewer supervisors, staff support people, and indirect employees than there are in traditional manufacturing situations. In one General Motors plant, for example, there are only 24 white-collar employees for a production-employee population of almost 500. This results in a substantially lower total labor cost for the organization. In an electronic service organization, management found it needed only one-half as many first-level supervisors after they organized teams. The teams took over many of the supervisors' tasks.

Estimates vary considerably concerning how much the cost of labor can be reduced through an effective organization-wide program of self-managing work groups. In new plants, estimates of 20 percent to 40 percent lower total production costs are common.

Decision making and work methods can also improve as a result of teams. The team-meeting format gives individuals a chance to discuss work methods and procedures. Because employees are cross-trained and have considerable information about the organization, they are often in an excellent position to suggest improvements and solve problems. Because of their superior knowledge and information, they are in a much better situation to problem solve than are quality-circle members.

Problems that might occur with self-managing teams are listed below. In most cases they are similar to those associated with job enrichment.

- Salary costs will go up.
- Training costs will go up.
- Additional support personnel may be needed for training.
- Unmet expectations for organizational change can occur.
- Resistance by middle management can be a problem.
- Resistance by staff support groups can occur.
- Unmet expectations for personal growth and development can occur.
- Conflict between participants and nonparticipants can be a significant problem if only a few teams are formed.
- Time is lost in team meetings, and decisions may be slow.

The salary costs are likely to be higher than with job enrichment when skill-based pay is used. Training costs are also likely to be higher than with job enrichment because group-process training takes time and is expensive. Finally, time-consuming meetings are needed but not job enrichment.

Practical Applications of Work Teams

Teams definitely do not fit all workers or work situations. First, positive results tend to occur only where the technology creates a kind of task interdependence that makes work teams an attractive approach. To cite extreme examples, teams do not make sense in the case of cross-country truckdrivers or telephone operators. Their work is technologically designed to be done by an individual. The situation, of course, is quite different for a chemical plant operator or a basketball player; in these cases, technology forces interdependence. I cite the basketball player because of an event that occurred in the first course I took on organizations. Pete Newell was a guest lecturer and he talked about teamwork and effectiveness. He had just coached the 1960 U.S. Olympic team to victory. Many still argue that it was the greatest collection of individuals to ever represent the United States in basketball (it included Jerry West, Jerry Lucas, and Oscar Robertson). After acknowledging the members' great talent, Newell made the point that a great team needs more than great talent. Each of the ballplayers on the team was used to having the ball 40 percent of the time. There simply were not enough basketballs for this to continue (at least not in the games!). Thus, he had to train a number of individuals for roles that recognized the interdependencies in basketball.

Often, work can be designed for either individuals or teams because there are moderate levels of interdependence. In these cases, I try to find out something about the people and the potential for changing the technology before recommending an approach to job design.

There is an individual difference factor that comes into play when groups are involved. It was stressed that individual job enrichment works best when individuals have needs for growth, achievement, and competence. These same needs must be present for teams to operate effectively, but, in addition, people need to value social interaction. Social isolates and people who reject groups and teams clearly do not fit in self-managing work teams and, as a result, not all members of an existing work force adapt well to the team concept.

A brief example can help illustrate the problem some individuals have with teams. Joe had always operated a particular machine and was quite good at it. When the plant where he worked organized teams, he refused to do other jobs and to attend team meetings. When asked why, he said he just wanted to be the best machine operator. Initially the team left him alone, but eventually they decided he was undermining the team. They warned him that if he did not change he would be fired for not doing his job. In their minds, his job consisted of attending meetings and doing other tasks. Joe refused to change and more warnings followed. After a little over a year the group fired Joe for not doing his job. Was this fair? Within the group concept, yes! Joe was significantly holding back the team and preventing others from learning the job he controlled; in short, he was not doing all of his job, only a part. To this day, I am sure Joe would say he was unfairly treated because his way of thinking about work had no room for the team concept. In a plant populated by Joes, team designs hardly make sense, but individual enrichment might work.

Sometimes the technology is more changeable than are the people. At the Motorola electronic assembly plant mentioned earlier, it was shown that the work could be done by either an assembly line or individually enriched jobs. My feeling was that it could also have been done by teams. In 1961 I visited Nonlinear Systems, a company that made electronic instruments. At that time, they had abandoned assembly lines and were using teams. They found that their product, digital volt meters, could be made by either teams or individuals. In fact, some teams chose to simply have individuals do an entire assembly because their members did not want to engage in team activities.

One additional example from the electronics field illustrates just how flexible electronic-assembly technology can be. I was working with a large computer firm when it decided to enter the personal computer business. Two separate groups worked on the design of the manufacturing facility for the personal computers, the plant management team and a group of manufacturing engineers on corporate staff. The management team devised a team-based assembly approach while the engineers developed an assembly line to build the same product. Both approaches were viable. The company ended up building it on an assembly line because the engineers got budget approval to buy the assembly-line technology. Before the management team realized what was happening, nearly $30 million had been committed and there was no turning back; the initial flexibility had been removed by the large capital investment.

Volvo has found that product design may also need to change to fit the work design. After Volvo started using work teams, it realized just how much the design of cars was influenced by a desire to make them easy to build on an assembly line. Work team assembly called not just for a different plant design, but also for a different product design, which they are gradually doing.

It should be added that positive results stem from work teams only when the group process is positive. Since this does not always happen, groups can be highly ineffective and can waste a considerable amount of time. Because of the importance of a good group process, organizations that use teams need to make group skills an important part of their selection process.

The complexities of group process have led some to recommend individual job enrichment rather than team design where work can be designed either way (Hackman and Oldham, 1980). That is, where the technology does not strongly call for teams, job enrichment should be the preferred approach because of the complexities and difficulties involved in developing effective group processes. This is sage advice but it may be a bit too conservative. Choosing individual job enrichment can limit the movement of power, information, knowledge, and skills. Further, it precludes the tremendous positive force that can come from group pressure and social rewards.

Durability and Dissemination

As with job enrichment and, to a degree, with quality circles, work teams often do not last in most traditionally managed organizations. There are, of course, examples to the contrary, but in most instances, it is true. The reasons for this are very similar to those for job enrichment and quality circles. They stem directly from the fact that teams are usually tried in a small portion of the organization and that they do not affect enough systems or enough people in the organization. Let us look first at the issue of their survival.

As was mentioned earlier, General Electric found that none of its more than a hundred self-managing work groups survived. Considerable opposition and pressure grew up in other parts of the organization. Specifically, it became clear that significant changes were needed in the manager's role and that many of the staff and support jobs would have to change if self-managing work teams became standard operating procedure. Many people in managerial, staff, and support positions did not like these changes and as a a result did not support continuation of the self-managing work groups or their dissemination. In addition, employees who were in adjacent work areas and who were being managed in a traditional way often liked what they saw with respect to teams and requested that they, too, be managed in this way. This often did not meet with the approval and acceptance of management and, as a result, the existence of the teams proved to be an irritant. It raised demands for changes that managers did not want to spread throughout the organization.

A similar scenario developed in a repeat of the British coal-mining study (Goodman, 1979). Teams were formed in part of a United States coal mine. They showed some initial success but eventually were eliminated because of the conflict that arose between them and the rest of the mine workers, who felt unfairly treated. It was a classic case of social comparison. The rest of the employees were happy until they saw how the teams were treated. They became jealous because they thought the teams got some advantages that they did not. In short, even though they were not objectively worse off they felt worse off.

The reasons for the lack of dissemination are very similar to those for lack of institutionalization. The successes that are often initially experienced when teams are started are easily discounted by managers in other work areas who prefer to maintain their traditional authority relationships with their work force. They point out that these ideas are not applicable to their work area because of differences in technology and the nature of the work force. Sometimes this is a correct observation, of course, and therefore, they are successfully able to resist dissemination.

It often becomes clear that if widespread dissemination is to take place significant changes have to be made in the pay system, the training system, the selection system, and so on, and this may not meet with a favorable reaction from the rest of the organization. This same point often leads to the demise of the original work teams, when they begin to ask for changes in other systems in the organization (such as pay, scheduling, and quality control) and the maintainers of these systems resist. Other members of the organization do not want their jobs or their systems changed. Because they feel threatened they become opponents of the team concept.

In summary, self-managing work teams often do not either institutionalize or disseminate in traditional organizations, despite the fact that they often meet with initial success. The demands that they make simply require more change than many managers are willing to voluntarily accept. The greatest strength of this approach is also its greatest weakness. Because it affects power, knowledge, information, and rewards, it is effective as well as threatening. For these reasons, it is difficult to disseminate and institutionalize teams in traditional organizations. On the other hand, teams can be the basic building block upon which a high-involvement organization is constructed. They have the potential to be highly effective if they fit the technology and the rest of the organization is designed to support them.

8

Union-Management Quality-of-Work-Life Programs

Union-management relationships in the United States have, by tradition and design, been adversarial. This adversarial relationship represents a way of moving power to the rank-and-file workers in an organization. The very structure of collective bargaining is designed to allow employees to influence such areas as pay, job structures, discipline, and working conditions.

The adversarial relationship is limited, however, in the areas that it allows employees to gain power. For example, it rarely gives them a chance to influence capital investment, business strategy, work methods, and planning and scheduling decisions. It also does little to move information to lower levels in an organization or to improve the skills and knowledge of lower-level employees. In fact, it often inhibits the downward flow of information because managers become concerned about sharing information that will harm their bargaining position. Although it moves rewards downward, in most cases it has not created systems in which rewards are directly tied to the success of the organization. In short, it leaves many features of traditional management practice unchanged, and thus, as a move toward employee involvement, it is limited.

Perhaps the most damaging criticism of the adversarial

119

approach is its relative inefficiency. Adversarial relationships involve great amounts of time and effort. They represent an enormous parallel structure since they require a union hierarchy as well as an organizational hierarchy. Of course, when they fail to produce a resolution of differences, strikes and labor stoppages result. Finally, differences between union and management that cannot be amicably resolved often end up in formal grievances, which are time-consuming and expensive.

For decades it has been suggested that a more cooperative union-management relationship would be advantageous to both parties (Walton and McKersie, 1965). Cooperation offers wider and more efficient employee involvement as well as more effective organizational performance. The United States has seen periods of labor-management cooperation. During World War II, labor-management cooperative committees were formed in a number of the defense industries. In general, they died after the war and until the early 1970s labor-management cooperation was more of an academic concept than a reality in the American workplace.

Things began to change in the early 1970s. At that point, two important events occurred that proved to be catalysts for the introduction of union-management cooperative projects in hundreds of workplaces. First, the United Automobile Workers of America (UAW) signed a contract with General Motors Corporation that called for cooperative quality-of-work-life (QWL) programs in that corporation. Second, a program was launched by the Institute for Social Research at the University of Michigan that called for starting union-management QWL projects around the country (Lawler and Ozley, 1979; Seashore, 1981). Both of these programs became operational and contributed multiple examples of union-management cooperation. They both chose the QWL label to stress the point that these projects were intended to do more than improve productivity. They were designed to improve all aspects of life at work. As was mentioned earlier, concern for employees' well-being was high during the early 1970s and QWL became an important national topic.

The mid-1970s saw a slow growth in union-management

cooperation. Along with Stanley Seashore and Theodore Mills, I had responsibility for initiating QWL projects for the University of Michigan program. It was tough going. Unions in particular were hesitant to be part of a project. We finally settled on a strategy of identifying an interested forward-looking union leader, such as Irv Bluestone of the UAW, and asking him what company he would like to work with on a QWL project. We then went to the company, assured of the union's interest. The reverse process, starting with management interest and then trying to get union support, simply did not work. The union officials were unwilling to go along with something that was company-initiated. Ultimately we started eight QWL projects in the mid-1970s.

The current momentum for the QWL movement was provided by the economic downturn and international competition that hit basic U.S. industries in the late 1970s and early 1980s. This, along with some societal forces mentioned earlier in this book, led to widespread proliferation of union-management QWL projects in the early 1980s.

Virtually every major union has become involved in at least one QWL project; the UAW and the Communication Workers of America have been particularly active. Most major corporations with unions have also become involved. To name just a few corporations, General Motors, Ford, Xerox, AT&T, and most steel companies have now become involved in QWL projects. The U.S. Department of Labor lists over a hundred cooperative union-management projects and, in response to their growth, the Labor Department itself has instituted a bureau to support and encourage them. Thanks to a happy coincidence of world events, some successful demonstration projects, and the leadership of people like Irv Bluestone, an idea that initially was supported by only a few people in the early 1970s has become a widespread practice within a decade (Cohen-Rosenthal, 1985).

As one of the original advocates of QWL, I was at first surprised by how difficult it was for it to gain acceptance, while today I am surprised by how fast it has spread. If anything, I am afraid that today the original model is too often seen as the ultimate approach to union-management relations. Despite its success, it has limitations. We need to increasingly focus on a second-generation high-involvement model of union-management relations. But before considering a second generation model we need to look in more detail at the basic QWL model.

Characteristics of QWL Projects

Most QWL projects now follow a well-developed and well-established model. Of course, each project ultimately defines its own structures, traditions, and approaches, but this is usually done within the context of a general model that includes the features described below.

Joint Committee Structure. A committee structure is at the core of most QWL projects. These committees form the cooperative bridge between the union and the organization. In essence, they are a parallel intervening structure between the union and the organization. They typically exist at multiple levels in the organization. In a large corporation, there is usually one at the highest level of the union and the management; for example, in both Ford and General Motors there is a corporate-level committee that includes corporate officers and union officials. There is also a committee at each major lower level until the plant level is reached. The plant-level committee typically spawns additional groups and participative activities in the plant.

The joint committee structure is responsible for providing the direction and impetus for a QWL program. The committees are expected to make it happen and are the key structural vehicle on which the entire program rests. The hierarchical nature of these committees reflects the reality that both the union and the organization are hierarchical. As with any hierarchical structure, different tasks are allocated to different levels in the organization. The top level provides general direction and support. At lower levels, specific activities are identified and changes are acted upon. The committees, like quality circles, represent a parallel structure—in this case, between the union organization and the work organization.

Letter of Agreement. The union and management typically sign a letter of agreement. Among other things, this letter usually says that no individuals will lose their jobs or pay as a result of the project and that the project will not deal with collective bargaining issues. The latter point is particularly important since it is often a very sensitive one for the union. Unions are concerned that QWL projects will undermine the collective bargaining arrangements that have been in operation for decades. Instead of undermining them, the QWL program is supposed to complement them by allowing the union to influence various decisions that are not influenced through collective bargaining. Letters also talk about the kind of committee structure to be created by the QWL program; state that the program is voluntary; and often set some general objectives for the program.

Objectives. QWL programs typically have three kinds of objectives—union objectives, management objectives, and joint objectives. Although most objectives are not specified as being primarily held by the union or by management, the reality is that both parties enter into QWL projects because they wish to accomplish specific things. For example, the union may wish to strengthen its position and popularity with the work force, to increase its membership by making the company more successful, and to provide a better work environment for the membership by increasing its influence in areas where it normally does not have much. Management may wish to reduce the adversarial relationship, to improve the collective bargaining process, and, of course, to improve organizational performance through higher productivity and higher quality.

The objectives of the program are usually stated in the letter of agreement and are widely disseminated to the participants. Often they are summarized into a few general statements, such as improving product quality and the quality of work life or increasing employee involvement. The programs at General Motors and Ford Motor Company, for example, stress improved product quality. At General Motors, the emphasis is on quality of work life as a method of improving product quality. Ford calls its program "employee involvement" and focuses on improved product quality. The 1980 basic steel agreement between the United Steel Workers of America and the major steel companies calls for employee participation teams to discuss and decide on means to improve performance, employee morale and dignity, and conditions of work.

Collective Bargaining Separate from QWL. As indicated by the letter of agreement, the collective bargaining process is kept separate from the QWL process. However, separation is never perfect because many of the same people who are involved in QWL committees are also involved in the collective bargaining process. In fact, when collective bargaining takes place, there may be a time conflict between QWL activities and the bargaining process. The same people have to spend scarce time on one or the other. Nevertheless, the formal agreement is that the two are separate activities.

Experimental Joint Projects or Programs. QWL programs typically start with experimental projects somewhere in the organization. Higher-level committees usually pick a plant or location that they feel is particularly attractive as a starting point and concentrate their resources there. In some cases, projects start at a plant without any top-level union or company involvement. This occurs where a company has a variety of unions and, thus, it can deal with each location on a separate basis. This situation has occurred at Miller Brewing Company, Flying Tiger Airline, and a host of other organizations. Ford and General Motors, on the other hand, have joined with the UAW to create corporate-wide programs and committee structures. In the case of Ford, their program began with a project in a large assembly plant at Indianapolis. This project ultimately led to the corporate-wide employee involvement program.

What occurs in experimental locations, of course, often determines how much the overall concept spreads to the rest of the corporation and what type of activities become associated with the term QWL. This was certainly true in the case of Ford. The initial success in Indianapolis encouraged the corporation to go ahead. Also, because the Indianapolis project successfully used problem-solving groups, they spread throughout the corporation. The widely publicized Tarrytown plant (Guest, 1979) seemed to have the same impact on General Motors.

QWL Training Program. The initial step in QWL programs

is a general training program for all participants. The work force at a plant, for example, is introduced to the general concept and objectives of QWL. Training in cooperative problem solving is provided, as is information about the business and the company. This initial training indicates the company's and the union's commitment to the project and represents the beginning of information sharing and skill building. Depending on the structure of the program, this training may take anywhere from a few hours to several days. Following it, specific changes are identified.

Change Areas. Responsibility for identifying specific changes rests with the QWL committees. There may be only one of these at a location, or many may be created, depending on the structure of the program. The most frequent approach is to create one or two QWL committees at each level in the organizational hierarchy. This often expands to create a structure similar to a quality-circle program, in which numerous shop floor problem-solving groups as well as some joint task forces are created to look at particular issues.

The type and number of joint problem-solving groups is the key design feature in any QWL project. It determines what type of projects and activities the program deals with. If numerous groups are created at the shop floor level, then the program typically looks like a quality-circle program. Jointly sponsored groups focus on improving work methods as well as working conditions. Training in work methods and procedures is a common activity. Similarly, groups often get involved in improving the physical surroundings, safety, and general working conditions. This is hardly surprising since safety has been a joint union-management concern for decades in many plants.

A few QWL programs have not created problem-solving groups. Instead they have decided to focus on organization-wide issues. They have gone beyond such things as training and work-environment improvements to deal with work standards, costs, bids, work planning, and purchasing and installation of new equipment. For example, in a QWL project in San Diego, changes were made in the purchase of trucks (Lawler and Ledford, 1982). In the highly publicized UAW-Harmon Industries project at Bolivar, Tennessee, a system for granting individuals time off when their work is done was developed. Typically, this kind of activity is sponsored by the higher-level joint committees.

Sometimes, QWL committees will deal with such ideas as gainsharing and may even look at such contractual issues as hours of work and work schedules. My research center at the University of Southern California is currently working with a company in which union and management cooperate in developing bids for new work and in changing work rules to make the organization more productive. Both sides have also cooperatively designed a method for sharing productivity gains. As part of the cooperative bidding process, the union has agreed to adjust wages in order to make the company competitive. These are difficult areas for QWL programs because they are contractual and, as such, not within the mandate of most QWL projects. In fact, dealing with these issues was so controversial in a forest products project that it contributed to the termination of the project by the union. As a result, QWL projects have rarely produced significant changes in collective bargaining issues. For example, QWL projects have rarely developed gainsharing plans or skill-based pay systems.

Third-Party Facilitator. Most QWL projects depend heavily on a third-party facilitator who helps define objectives, provides training, and does group-process facilitation. In the case of General Motors, these people are typically employed by the company. In most cases, however, they are private consultants who specialize in QWL programs. Before the mid-1970s, few of these experts were available in the United States. However, the number has grown tremendously in the last decade, and there are now numerous facilitators and consultants as well as local joint union-management groups that can recommend facilitators and provide training. Some states, such as Michigan, have QWL centers that provide technical assistance.

In summary, QWL projects have a number of common features, but each tends to take on its own character and develop its own agenda. This is particularly true when the action moves to a particular plant or worksite. Here, depending on the history of the union-management relationship, the type of business, and the organization, the project may focus on creating a quality-circle structure, or it may create task forces to deal with particularly pressing problems, to mention just two alternatives. Thus, knowing that a company has a QWL project provides some general information about what they are doing but does not specify in any detail what kind of change is taking place. It also says little about how effective it is.

Schedule of Events: QWL Program

The sequence of events in the start-up of the QWL program is generally consistent from one project to another. QWL programs usually begin with separate education of the union and of management. Here the third-party consultant highlights the advantages of creating these programs to both parties. Clearly, in order for a project to start, both parties have to see that it is in their best interest. In many cases, the traditional adversarial relationship has served both parties quite well for decades; thus, they may not be receptive to a new approach. The leadership on both sides may be particularly comfortable with the old way. It has gotten them into power, kept them there, and they know how to relate in an adversarial manner. They may see even a small change as quite threatening.

One of my biggest surprises when I started work on QWL projects was the resistance by the labor-relations executives in corporations. I naively assumed that they would welcome QWL projects as a way out of an unpleasant adversary process. What I failed to recognize was that the process had served them well: it had brought them to positions of considerable power and was an important basis for their continuing power. In effect, they told the rest of the organization that they were indispensable to companies successfully dealing with the union, just as accountants are needed to deal with taxes.

If both parties see QWL as viable, the next step is to convene them into a joint team-building session in which the ground rules for the program are developed and goals are set. This usually takes several days. A letter of agreement based on the results of this meeting is developed and is usually signed by both parties. Following the team building and letter of agreement, the joint committee structure is created, whereby both sides identify their participants. In most cases, these reflect the existing hierarchy; that is, union leaders and top management are on the top-level committee and so on down. The union sometimes appoints nonofficers to its committees, but this is rare.

Following the creation of this structure, team building and training takes place for the members of the committees as well as for the work force in general. This training is interpersonal, group-process oriented, and problem-solving oriented. Following the training, an organizational diagnosis is typically done. This may be a formal diagnosis using questionnaires and interviews, or it may be very short, relying on existing information.

Following diagnosis, experimental change projects are identified. As mentioned above, these may be training programs, the proliferation of quality circles in the organization, or a host of other possible projects.

If these changes go well, they are institutionalized, along with the QWL committee structure itself—they become a regular part of the ongoing operation of the organization. Some of the original projects are now over ten years old and the joint committees continue to meet regularly. Similarly, some of the earliest changes having to do with joint problem solving through team meetings and new work methods remain in place.

QWL Program Effects on Participation

The effects of QWL projects on power, information, rewards, and knowledge are limited by the parallel structure of the programs. Nevertheless, they do have an effect. Let us look at each of them separately.

Power. The effects on power are somewhat subtle but, nevertheless, significant. First, it is important to remember that QWL committees are usually prohibited from discussing bargaining issues. This is not to say, of course, that they do not sometimes discuss them; they often do and this can be a controversial feature of QWL programs. Second, they typically have no formal power to decide things. In essence, they are expected to make recommendations to the existing power structure about the kinds of changes that are desirable. As such, their power is very much a function of the quality of the recommendations that they make and, of course, their ability to persuade the existing power structure of the wisdom of their ideas. Part of the key to the power of the QWL program can be found in the membership on the QWL committees. If members are representatives of the key power groups of the organization, then it is highly probable that QWL committee recommendations will be implemented.

Most consultants who set up QWL programs emphasize the importance of having the key power groups in the organizations well represented in the QWL committee structure. For example, it is recommended that at the corporate level and at the local plant, the key management person be involved. Similarly, it is usually recommended that at the plant level, the local union leadership be heavily represented on the joint committee structure. This is a formal recognition of the fact that in order to be successful the "powerless" QWL committee structure must have direct links to the individuals who can make decisions. Indeed, it is probably fair to say that the major power of QWL programs rests in their bringing together key union and management people to discuss issues that are not traditionally addressed by them.

Because the QWL committee structure involves high-level managers and union officials, QWL programs typically have more effect on power than do quality-circle programs. The union is present and it can follow up on ideas and changes to see if they are implemented; no comparable group exists in most quality-circle programs. The weakness in QWL programs is that they do little to directly shift power to lower levels in the organization. In effect, they are a move to representative democracy, with the union officials in the role of spokespersons for the work force.

Information. One of the more successful objectives of most QWL programs is to share business information more widely in the organization. This is particularly likely to happen when task forces are created to deal with such business issues as the purchase of new machinery, problems with suppliers, costs, causes of poor-quality products, and the making of bids and proposals for new business. The major impact of a QWL project is often in the area of information sharing. In many, but not all cases, the creation of committee structures and task forces causes an array of communication channels to open. As a result, people often come to understand the business better and to participate more effectively in problem-solving activities.

Rewards. QWL programs do little to affect extrinsic rewards. This is largely because they are not allowed to deal with contractual issues. A few programs have gone into gainsharing, which is often set up aside from the collective bargaining agreement. More typical is the following situation that I encountered. Several problem-solving groups suggested to the top-level QWL committee that a gainsharing plan be developed. It was discussed briefly and dropped because the union leader insisted that it was a bargaining issue and had to be handled within the contract. The organization tried to do this at a later date but failed, largely because of the difficulty of developing a gainsharing plan in an adversarial mode.

Some QWL programs have developed changes in pay and promotion practices that have ultimately been incorporated into the contract. For example, in some of General Motors' new plants, skill-based pay has been instituted partially as a result of the QWL programs.

Knowledge. QWL projects typically increase the skills and knowledge of a significant number of people in the organization. Typically, the primary beneficiaries are the people who end up on the QWL committees. They often receive interpersonal and group-skill training as well as training in decision making. Less training is usually done for other members of the organization, but they are certainly not ignored. As was mentioned earlier, a plant-wide organizational training program that everyone participates in typically introduces the program. Additional training may be provided to members of the work force as a result of the specific recommendations of the QWL committees. It is common, for example, to find that QWL committees recommend specific training in such things as quality control, work methods and procedures, and supervisory behavior. Thus, in general, QWL programs result in additional knowledge and skills being developed.

In summary, QWL programs generally change the power relationships and the information that is generally available in the organization as well as the knowledge and skills of the work force. QWL programs generally have a moderate impact in all of these areas. Since, in most cases, they cannot directly affect collective bargaining procedures, they are unable to significantly alter a number of important things, including job structures and reward systems. Thus, they usually do not affect all the systems in an organization and therefore cannot create a truly consistent participative approach to organizing and managing people. This can be done only if the contract is altered.

On the positive side, QWL projects often produce changes that affect everyone in an organization. Much of the credit for this usually goes to the union because it is the first to raise issues of equality of treatment. Although a new practice may be tried with a few people, it is shortly either eliminated or spread throughout the organization. A good example of this came up in the Bolivar project. An experiment was tried in which employees were allowed to have free time once they had met their production standards. It was very successful with the work group that initially tried it. Pressure immediately developed to make it an organization-wide policy. This was done even though it did not fit some of the other work areas in the plant as well as it fit the original one.

This case also points to the one group that sometimes is overlooked in QWL projects—the white collar employees. They were never successfully included in the free-time program nor in some of the other QWL activities. This is hardly surprising since they are usually not well represented in the QWL committee structures.

Results of QWL Projects

QWL projects have the potential to produce a number of positive changes, such as improving the quality of life so that the organization becomes a more satisfying and meaningful place to work, increasing the operating effectiveness of the unit where the project takes place, and improving the nature of the union-management relationship. Of course, none of these changes is independent of each other. As previously mentioned, changes in people's satisfaction are indirectly related to organizational effectiveness. Also, changes in the nature of the union and its relationship to management can affect the long-term effectiveness of the organization.

The literature on QWL programs is full of positive reports about the success of these projects. Some projects, such as those at General Motors, Tarrytown, New York,(Guest, 1979) and some of the Ford projects (Copenhaver and Guest, 1982), have become major examples of how unions and management can relate together in new and positive ways (Simmons and Mares, 1983). General Motors attributed its success in obtaining local union contracts during its 1981 negotiations directly to the presence of QWL projects in its plants. On the other hand, a number of projects have failed and have been abandoned. At present, there are no accurate data on the success rate of QWL projects. In fact, only a handful of projects have been systematically studied to determine their impact (see, for example, Goodman, 1979; Hanlon, Nadler, and Gladstein, 1985; Nurick, 1985). Unquestionably, the best-studied projects are those that were part of the original University of Michigan QWL program. They were subject to an extensive measurement program and, therefore, we have fairly good data on their success rate (Lawler and Ledford, 1982). In the case of most other projects, we have to rely on post hoc case descriptions of what went on or on the reports of participants.

In reviewing the results of the projects, we will look at the different areas that they are likely to affect. Thus, we will separately consider their impact on employee satisfaction and well-being, productivity, and the union-management relationship.

Employee Satisfaction

QWL projects rather consistently improve employee well-being and satisfaction. This is an important goal, which is usually reached because of the kinds of activities the projects install.

It is common for QWL programs to recommend the start-up of problem-solving groups such as quality circles because this involves a number of people and rarely do people object to the creation of these groups. At least initially, as we noted in our discussion of quality circles, this has a positive impact and people are eager to volunteer. Group membership in task forces and problem-solving groups can be particularly satisfying when they take on and solve major organizational issues. I have seen task forces develop bids for new business, solve major quality problems, and make important purchasing decisions. When this occurs, the psychological rewards for the participants are considerable. For example, an attitude survey at Ford in locations with a QWL program found employees were more satisfied as a result of their being involved in the thinking side of their work.

QWL committees often recommend changes in the workplace that are desired by employees. In particular, they make changes in the physical environment: parking lots, cafeterias, restrooms, and time clocks. There are usually two reasons why QWL projects focus on working conditions. First, many managers, union leaders, and employees believe that satisfaction leads to productivity. Hence, project leaders try to find ways of making the organization a more satisfying workplace. Second, it is often easier to create a more pleasant work environment than it is to change management styles, job design, patterns of coordination and communication, and reward systems. Suggestions for improving physical work conditions are easy to generate, since making the suggestions requires no special expertise and such problems are usually highly visible—anyone can see the need for a bigger parking lot. On the other hand, problems with the way the work is performed are usually complex and difficult to solve.

If changes are implemented in job design, work methods, and work coordination, there is often an improvement in satisfaction. As was noted earlier, people find it satisfying to work in an effective organization, where jobs are interesting and challenging. Sometimes the grievance procedures become smoother and the adversarial relationship is reduced because of QWL projects. In the case of General Motors' Tarrytown facility, the drop was from 2,000 outstanding grievances in 1972 to 32 in 1978. Grievances at Marathon Steel dropped from 318 to 117 over a one-year period. This, of course, can lead to greater satisfaction for individual parties as their particular issues get dealt with more swiftly and more effectively. Finally, it is hardly satisfying to work in an environment where two parties are at each other's throats constantly. QWL programs can also affect satisfaction by leading to employees' being treated with more respect and dignity. One indirect measure of this is provided by the work of Karen Cornelius at Ford, who has kept track of language changes that have occurred during Ford's QWL program. She has noted that in the past, people were referred to as "heads," "the troops," and "sheep" while management was said to "take names and kick ass," "point fingers," and "practice mushroom management" (keep them in the dark and throw manure on them). New terms include "human resources," "two-way communication," "our people," and "walk your talk."

In summary, although the reasons are varied, it seems likely that QWL projects lead to improved employee well-being and job satisfaction. This is supported by surveys at General Motors and Ford that show an increase in employee satisfaction and an inclination to continue QWL projects. For example, in a recent survey at Ford, over 90 percent of the employees said that the QWL project was a good idea that should be continued. Similar data has been found by University of Michigan QWL surveys. Thus, it seems safe to assume that QWL programs usually increase employee satisfaction and well-being.

Organizational Effectiveness

Very few case histories show the long-term effects of QWL programs on productivity or organizational effectiveness. Unless programs directly focus on improving productivity or quality through changing communication patterns, employee skills, or employee motivation, they are unlikely to directly affect organizational performance. There are a number of reasons why improving employee satisfaction through better working conditions may not improve productivity.

First, as was noted earlier, the simplistic belief that satisfaction leads to productivity is wrong. Thus, even though improvements in the workplace increase satisfaction, increases in productivity and organizational effectiveness may not occur. Some long-term gains may be expected because of lower turnover, fewer strikes, fewer grievances, and less absenteeism. But companies measure financial performance and productivity in short-term gains. Thus, increases in satisfaction may not have a detectable impact on the bottom line.

Second, implementing changes in the work environment often takes longer than many expect. Major construction projects can take months or even years, and delays are common. In addition, changes in the work environment often require several financial approvals, thus making management appear cumbersome and unsympathetic. During a long delay in making these changes, employees and managers may come to view the QWL program as a failure and it may be abandoned before it even has a chance to improve productivity.

Third, the cost of improvements in the work environment often far exceeds the benefits in productivity. Even if a better work environment does translate into higher productivity and other organizational benefits, the benefits are almost always small. The cost of building a new cafeteria or air conditioning a work area, for example, are rarely, if ever, recouped. As a result, managers may come to see QWL as a costly or futile program with no benefits to the organization and thus may lose interest in it.

This does not mean, however, that working conditions should be ignored entirely. It may be necessary to improve working conditions in order to win credibility for a new program. Particularly if a work environment is dangerous or extremely uncomfortable, employees may not trust management's motivation unless improvements are made. In addition, certain improvements in the work environment have potential benefits for both productivity and the employees. In particular, safety and health improvements can benefit both employees and the organization. Finally, there is a social responsibility to provide good working conditions. For this reason, making the workplace pleasant ought to be pursued as an end in itself rather than as a means to productivity improvement.

Overall more than amenities and employee satisfaction must be sought if organizational effectiveness is to improve. Changes in work methods, procedures, pay, and job design must be achieved. This, of course, raises the question of how likely achievement of these changes is.

Although the evidence is incomplete, records from those QWL projects that have been carefully documented indicate that productivity improvements can be obtained through QWL programs. However, only two of the eight original Michigan program sites showed clear impacts on productivity (Lawler and Ledford, 1982). In some of the organizations, productivity was difficult or impossible to measure, so no conclusions could be reached. In other cases, there were no improvements simply because nothing was changed that affects productivity.

In the many cases that have not been systematically studied, there are claims of tremendous improvements in product quality as a result of QWL programs. Since product quality directly contributes to productivity and to financial performance, improvements in quality can satisfy management and financially justify the continuation of a QWL program. Ford, for example, claims that its QWL program has contributed substantially to product quality improvements. One report of the Ford Sharonville plant's QWL effort states that customer complaints dropped by 70 percent. Attitude survey work at Ford also supports the argument for improved quality. Before the QWL program, 54 percent of the employees rated quality as excellent, while afterward, this figure rose to 72 percent.

Given the possible quality improvements, it is not surprising that improved performance has been reported as a result of QWL programs. For example, the General Motors' Tarrytown plant went from sixteenth out of eighteen General Motors' plants to first place on their internal measures. Ford's Sharonville plant showed annual cost improvements of almost 7.5 percent for 1980 through 1984 (whereas 2.5 percent was common during this time period for other Ford plants).

The degree to which a QWL program can improve organizational effectiveness is limited by the fact that the contract itself cannot be directly affected by the program. Contracts can prevent elimination of work rules that stop people from doing their own maintenance, for example, and contracts can prevent people being cross-trained and functioning in self-managing teams. Thus, some obvious approaches to improved productivity may be ruled out.

Although no reduction in support or supervisory staff is likely because of QWL programs, there are chances for improvement, particularly in areas of employee skills, knowledge, and understanding of the business as well as the work flow. Also, such counterproductive behaviors as grievances, absenteeism, and turnover can be reduced as a result of QWL projects. Quality improvements seem to be particularly likely, as highlighted in Ford's television commercials that point to a large increase in quality.

In several respects, it is not surprising that improved quality is an outcome of these projects. First, it is a goal both union and management share. (Productivity increases, on the other hand, smack of "speedup" and are seen as management's issue.) In addition, our earlier review of the research on motivation and participation pointed out that when people feel responsible for something, they want to do a high-quality job; thus, they are willing to improve work methods and pay more attention to quality.

In summary, possible improvements from QWL programs are listed below.

- Work-methods procedures may improve because of problem-solving groups.
- Attraction and retention will improve in most cases.
- Staffing flexibility is not affected unless it is the target of the training.
- Quality may improve because of motivation and methods.

- Rate of output may improve slightly.
- Grievances are likely to be reduced.
- Decision making may improve.
- Employees' skills are likely to improve.

As can be seen, QWL projects are expensive to operate and thus, in order to get a payoff in net productivity and organizational effectiveness, have to produce significant gains or savings. Accurate cost estimates for QWL programs are almost completely missing. A study by Goodman (1979) is a rare exception. Another exception is an estimate for the training program at Tarrytown of $1.6 million (Guest, 1979). In addition to training, the heavy operating cost is due to the fact that QWL programs represent a parallel structure to the existing one and thus require extra people and involve considerable cost time for meetings, training, and other support activities.

Possible negative consequences from QWL programs are listed below.

- Salary costs can increase.
- Training costs will increase.
- Support personnel will increase.
- Unmet expectations for organizational change are likely.
- Resistance by middle management is likely to occur since its jobs are often negatively affected.
- Resistance by staff support groups is likely to occur since their jobs are negatively affected.
- Unmet expectations for personal growth are likely.
- Production time is lost in meetings, and decision making can be slow.

It is also important to note that of the eight original QWL projects started as part of the union-management program at the University of Michigan, only one lasted more than five years. In some cases, the companies and unions have gone on to start other QWL projects and are committed to the process even though the initial project has faded. Where the projects were cancelled, sometimes the union and sometimes management was the cause. Unions tended to withdraw when the QWL program threatened the adversarial relationship and the power base of the union leadership. When management withdrew, it typically was because they found the time and cost greater than the returns.

The financial impact of QWL programs is multifaceted. They by no means produce a guaranteed positive impact on organizational effectiveness. In fact, the direct impact may never be a major one. Much of their financial justification must come through their indirect impact: the positive effects they have on employee satisfaction and well-being and the union-management relationship. Also, if QWL projects do focus on changes that affect productivity, then it is likely that they will have a positive impact on productivity and organizational effectiveness.

Union-Management Relationships

There are numerous reports of QWL projects improving the basic relationship between the union and management. These reports typically focus on reduced grievance rates and on easier and more pleasant contract negotiations, such as the case of General Motors' new car company, Saturn. As part of this project, management has developed a unique cooperative agreement with the UAW. Although it cannot be proven, it seems highly unlikely that the Saturn agreement could have been reached without the decade of QWL activity that preceded it.

Better union-management relationships can profit and benefit both the union and management. It can be a tremendous cost-saver if it reduces the likelihood of strikes or grievances and facilitates change. QWL projects may indirectly influence the kinds of provisions that are put in contracts, as in the case of General Motors, where contracts with UAW that cover new plants include certain QWL-type provisions. For example, pay for skills is included specifically as a result of QWL activities. Similarly, job descriptions are more flexible and manning levels are quite different in these new plants as a result of the joint QWL activities that have been so prominent at General Motors over the last ten years.

Less obvious examples have occurred at local plants, where the QWL process has facilitated contract changes that improve product quality and employee well-being. Even though QWL programs are formally kept separate from collective bargaining, there is bound to be some mutual influence. Just as QWL programs tend to slow down and lose initiative while the adversarial collective bargaining process is taking place, the adversarial process has to be influenced by the ideas, improvements, and changes that result from the QWL process.

Finally, it is worth noting that QWL projects often have an impact on the union itself, with respect to its structure and leadership style. In a number of cases, support of the QWL program has become an issue in union politics. So far, union leaders who support QWL projects generally gain in popularity and power because they are seen as leading the union in a positive direction. Survey results from Ford show that 91 percent of participants in problem-solving groups and 80 percent of non-participants think that the union was right to get involved in QWL. Glenn Watts, then president of the Communication Workers of America, noted that the start-up of the AT&T effort, though radical, was warmly received by the members of the union (Simmons and Mares, 1983).

Nevertheless, some union leaders clearly see QWL projects as threats to their power base, particularly when they have built their power on an adversarial relationship and grievances (which are reduced in the QWL process). In several cases, this has led unions to withdraw from QWL projects. One of the first union leaders I met who was threatened by a QWL project had always run his local in an autocratic, secretive way. He started a QWL project because he wanted the visibility within the union movement that it offered. (If I had known this in advance, I never would have been involved in starting the project.) All went well until the union members stated that the union local should be run according to QWL principles. Once this happened, he began looking for a way to end the union's involvement.

In general, union officers who have led their memberships into QWL programs have found themselves and their union strengthened as a result of these programs. Of course, one biasing factor here is that traditionally adversarial union leaders simply do not enter QWL projects and, as a result, do not find themselves threatened by them. For example, the machinist's union has been adamantly opposed to QWL projects and, as a result, has not had to face the issue of losing its adversarial power base because of a successful QWL program.

Conditions for Success

Some research has been done to determine conditions favorable to the success of QWL projects (Nadler, Hanlon, and Lawler, 1980). In general, the following conditions seem to be critical for effective QWL projects:

- The project must be owned by the key power groups in the organizations. The top union people and the top management people have to see it as their project and have to be committed to its success.
- The goals of the project need to be clear and generally accepted. This means that there has to be a vision of what the project is about, and the vision must be widely shared and accepted.
- The consultant must be effective. Particularly important here is a consultant who can relate effectively to both the union and management and not be seen as biased or partial toward one or the other. In addition, of course, the consultant needs the skills to facilitate group process, clarify goals and directions, and suggest various problem solutions.
- The various labor-management committees need to function effectively. This usually means that they need good training in problem solving, and they need leadership that allows exploration of the evidence and good decision making to take place. In addition, committees must be clear about their role and must have the opportunity to deal with critical issues. Openness and trust within the committees are also important. This usually comes about only when good team building has taken place and the individual members can put aside

their traditional roles and commit themselves to making the committees successful.

- The general organizational climate must be supportive of the program. Successful programs are most likely to come about in organizations where good union-management relations already exist and where both the union leadership and management are secure. Related to this is the willingness and the capability of the organization to handle change. When an organization is change-oriented and people are secure, successful projects are likely.

- Less important, but also sometimes contributing to failure, is the economic situation in the organization. Often, an adverse financial situation makes it difficult to get a union-management project started. There are a number of features of a struggling company that make it difficult to find the time and money to support a QWL project. This is somewhat opposed to the common-sense view that labor and management cooperate only in desperate situations. It is true that problems can bring them together for joint action, but a desperate situation does not assure success.

Future of QWL Programs

It is difficult to reach any final conclusion concerning the effectiveness of most union-management QWL programs. Many are still in their early stages and, to a significant degree, most organizations are still learning how to utilize the framework of QWL programs. Nevertheless, they represent a promising alternative or additional way for unions and management to relate to each other. They are particularly likely to improve the general working conditions and the well-being of employees. As we noted earlier, they are less likely to improve productivity and operating effectiveness. Nevertheless, a number of organizations have used them to improve product quality and have reduced such counterproductive behaviors as grievances, strikes, absenteeism, and turnover.

With the exception of the Scanlon Plan and some other forms of gainsharing (to be discussed in the next chapter), QWL projects represent the only established way for union and management to create a more participative work culture and organization. Thus, even though the results at this point are mixed and these projects are difficult to manage and implement, they do represent the best starting point for labor-management cooperation.

Perhaps the best way to think of them is as the first step in a long-term transition in the union-management relationship. They represent the crawling stage that ultimately progresses to walking and running. I think of them as the crawling stage because of their limited impact on power, knowledge, information, and rewards. As long as they operate outside collective bargaining, their impact will remain limited.

However, the Saturn project has shown that it is possible to make the transition to the next stage, which involves more participation. If this transition goes well, some of the extra cost can be eliminated and ultimately the union and management can enter into a more participative and truly jointly involved relationship.

When I originally worked with others on the QWL committee-structure model, I never thought of it as a permanent parallel structure. Instead, I thought of it as a way to change the organization's normal way of doing business. The key to deeper long-term change is to get committees to change the organization to a new form of participation. This new form should increase the areas that can be affected by the QWL program to include contractual items. It probably should create an open contract that is continuously improved upon through the QWL committee structure. One QWL project in the steel industry has already reached this point and it is possible that others will follow. This kind of union-management relationship can, in fact, be highly supportive of the type of high-involvement management in which people care more, know more, and do more in the workplace.

9

Gainsharing

The term *gainsharing* is relatively new. The idea of paying a bonus to employees based on improvements in the operating results of an organization, however, is old and well-established one. Many different formulas exist for calculating payouts based on improvements in organizational performance. In most cases (such as the typical profit-sharing plan), these formulas are part of economic incentive plans and are not tied into a management philosophy that is consistent with or part of a participative-management effort. A notable exception is a gainsharing plan known as the Scanlon Plan. It is as much a participative-management program as it is an incentive plan.

The Scanlon Plan dates back to the 1930s and today enjoys increasing acceptance (see, for example, Lesieur, 1958; Moore and Ross, 1978). Another classic plan is the Lincoln Electric Plan. It, too, dates back more than forty years. Other currently popular gainsharing plans include the Improshare Plan and the Rucker Plan.

Until recently, gainsharing plans existed primarily in small privately owned companies. Two of the best-known ones are in the Donnelly Mirror Company and the Herman Miller Company, two relatively small companies. Recently, a number of large corporations have installed them in some of their plants. For example, General Electric, Goodyear, TRW, Motorola, and Mead have one or more gainsharing plans in their plants.

Gainsharing plans are particularly important because of the direct connection that they establish between participative management and financial bonus programs. This is particularly true in the case of the Scanlon Plan, which has argued from the beginning that it is impossible to separate psychological participation from financial participation in the success of the business (Lesieur, 1958). Because of its strong emphasis on this point, it does quite a bit to move information, knowledge, rewards, and power to the lower levels of an organization. Unlike all the approaches discussed so far, it consistently affects rewards in an important way: it moves financial information and financial rewards for organizational performance to the lowest levels of the organization.

It is beyond the scope of this book to go into a detailed discussion of the different gainsharing plans. We will, however, describe the general characteristics of gainsharing plans, look at the results of the Scanlon Plan in some detail, briefly mention other well-known plans, and summarize the advantages and disadvantages of gainsharing plans.

Design Process

The first decision that an organization faces in setting up a gainsharing plan is how to design it. Gainsharing plans depend heavily on employee acceptance, input, and cooperation to make them work. This, in turn, depends on a high level of trust and understanding on the part of the employees. In most situations trust is difficult to achieve when the plan is management-owned and management-initiated. Hence, most consultants who install gainsharing recommend using a participative-design process, since it leads to acceptance, understanding, and high-quality decisions. The typical participative-design approach takes the form of a design committee that draws its members from all levels and parts of the organization. Members are trained and given the responsibility for designing the plan.

The only viable alternative to participative design is the use of a standardized plan and a trusted third party. For example, in many Scanlon Plan and Improshare Plan installations, the details of the plan are developed by a third party with the support of the union leadership and management. It is then voted on by the work force.

Organizational Unit Covered

The size of the organizational unit that is covered by a gainsharing plan varies widely, from companies with thousands of employees (Herman Miller, for example) to small plants or departments with less than fifty employees (Motorola, for example). In many situations, it is obvious what the appropriate unit is for a gainsharing plan. This is true, for example, in the case of a freestanding plant with good performance measurement and an employee population of less than five hundred. In these cases, a plan that covers the whole plant normally works well since it allows for good performance measurement and is usually small enough for individuals to see the relationship between their behavior and the bonus amount (what I will call line of sight). This is an important point. For the bonus to be motivating, the individual must be able to see a performance-reward connection.

The situation is much less clear when several plants exist on the same piece of land or when a single plant or operation exceeds five hundred employees. Under these conditions, there are advantages to installing two or more gainsharing plans. The primary advantage lies in bonuses that are more closely tied to the performance of individuals. However, there are significant problems with the idea of having multiple plans in the same plant or in several plants on a single plot of land. In both cases, the potential exists for significant conflict between people on different plans. This can be particularly debilitating when the people are technologically interdependent.

In the case of the single large plant, there also may be a

problem with the types of measures that exist for subunits of the plant. An exception to this are new plants that are structured around the mini-business concept. Sometimes these plants are divided into several businesses, each with its own economic information. This structure lends itself to multiple gainsharing plans in the same plant. This approach has allowed Motorola to provide over 80 percent of its manufacturing work force with a gainsharing plan. To the best of my knowledge, this represents the highest gainsharing coverage of any major U.S. corporation.

Determining the Bonus

All gainsharing plans are based on a formula for producing a bonus pool. The pool is divided among the members of the plan. A few general rules about the nature of the formula exist, but, to a large extent, formulas are custom designed. One way to think about the issues involved in developing a formula is to use the analogy of par for a golf course. Par is based on a consensus of what good performance is. When an individual beats this standard of performance, there has been a saving of strokes. When an individual performs worse than the standard, there has been a loss of strokes. Gainsharing plans basically work on the same principle. A par or standard is established. When the standard is improved on so that fewer costs are incurred, a bonus pool is available for sharing. When performance is worse than par, so that more costs are incurred, no bonus is available and an actual loss in the plan occurs.

A critical issue in establishing a gainsharing plan is where to set the goal or par. Other issues involve how the bonus pool will be divided once it is determined, how frequently performance will be measured for bonus purposes, what costs should be included, and how radical changes in the environment and in the organization will be handled. A brief review of each of these follows.

Developing a Goal or Standard. Most gainsharing plans start with the assumption that the standard should be based on history. They assume that both past pay and past performance have been fair and that if performance improves, so should pay.

They simply take a period of past performance, be it one, two, or more years, and say that improvements over that period will be shared. This approach is taken in the hope of avoiding a long and acrimonious debate over what is a fair standard. It also eliminates debate over how well the organization "should" be performing and what is "good performance." History has the obvious advantage of being a matter of record and, therefore, objective.

Unfortunately, the use of a historical standard does not always work since technological changes and environmental changes may outdate past operating results. A company may not be able to afford to use history if its past historical performance has been very poor and noncompetitive. Also, in new organizations, there is no long history of operating results on which to base a standard. If an adequate historical standard does not exist, then one option is to go with an engineered or estimated standard; another is to go with a standard that is changed over time.

Costs Covered. The Scanlon Plan and the Improshare Plan focus on labor costs. This is based on the view that labor costs are the most controllable costs in an organization. Since the idea is to motivate people and reward them for their performance, it makes sense to focus on costs that can be controlled, and labor costs typically can be controlled by employees.

The problem with focusing on labor costs is that they are only a small part of the total cost of many products and services, and they are not the only costs that employees can influence. Employees can often influence the cost of materials and supplies for example, and even utility costs. Not surprisingly, some organizations that have started with a pure Scanlon-Plan-type labor-cost formula have over the years added more and more costs to their bonus calculations.

A good example of adding costs or measures is the Donnelly Mirrors "Scanlon Plan," which in fact has become a profit-sharing plan that includes all of its costs in the bonus formula. It became a profit-sharing plan because employees found that they could reduce labor costs by using more materials and supplies. One of their supplies, diamond grinding wheels, is very expensive. Its use is directly related to how fast machines are run and to the willingness of employees to get the job done with a used wheel. The original labor-only gainsharing plan encouraged employees to run their machines at high speeds and to discard wheels as soon as they were worn, because this led to more units being produced by each worker. However, it also led to higher supply costs. Thus, the company found itself paying out bonuses without reducing *total* costs.

It does not follow, however, that a plan should start with all costs included. A strong argument can be made for starting with a simple plan and adding more costs as employees understand how they can reduce costs and begin to understand and trust the plan. This is precisely what Donnelly did. Most profit-sharing plans do not start this way. They start by covering all costs and often suffer from employees' not understanding them and not knowing how to influence them.

Sharing Gains. When gains are realized, plans differ in how these gains are shared. First, there is the issue of how much goes to the company or the ownership and how much goes to employees. There is no easy answer to the question of what is the best split between the organization and the employees. It can only be determined when it is known which costs are going to be included in the plan. In short, you need to know what is going to be in the pool before a logical decision can be made about splitting it up. In plans I have studied, the number varies from 0 percent for the company and 100 percent for employees to 30 percent for employees and 70 percent for the company. Neither approach is necessarily right or wrong. For example, although it might seem that the company gains nothing when it gets 0 percent, nothing could be further from the truth. In one case, a number of gains from higher productivity (savings in fringe benefits, deferred plant expansion, and utilities) simply were not put into the pool, as only cash labor savings went in.

As a general rule, in situations where a number of costs are included, it makes sense to have the organization's share be larger. In those situations where few costs are included, minimizing the organization's share is important in order for the program to generate enough reward for the employees. Incidentally, there is little research to guide us in determining just how large a bonus needs to be in order to be motivating. In my experience, at least 5 percent is needed to get people interested in a gainsharing plan.

The second decision that has to be made about dividing the bonus pool concerns who will share in the bonus. Most plans cover all employees in the organizational unit that is measured. The strong case for doing this emphasizes that everyone has an influence on organizational effectiveness and that traditional differences, such as office/factory and management/nonmanagement, need to be transcended if a bonus is to be earned. In some plans, however, top management has been left out, as have staff and office employees. Special circumstances (such as existing management bonus systems) sometimes justify this, but it is not advisable since it can set up a conflict between those who are on the plan and those who are not.

The third decision concerning sharing regards how the money will be divided among the employees. In most plans, this is a straight percentage of total salary. In other words, no effort is made to reach individual decisions about how much each employee should get. An exception to this is the Lincoln Electric Plan. In it, individual payment decisions are made. The result is that some individuals do much better than others in a given performance period. From a motivational point of view, this is a highly effective approach if the performance appraisal process can be done in a credible and valid way. However, it is not done in most cases because good performance measures are not available and because the focus is on producing cooperation and teamwork, not individual excellence.

Frequency of Bonus. The most frequently used period for bonus calculation is one month. This is an attractive time period because it often fits organizational records, and it is frequent enough to attract the attention of individuals. Conditions that favor a longer payout period include a highly seasonal business and a long production or billing cycle for a product or service. In these cases, month-to-month performance measures might prove to be erratic and an unreasonable basis for bonus payout. As a fall-back position, quarterly payments can be made.

Managing Change. Changes within and outside of organizations that affect the viability of gainsharing plans are constantly taking place. For example, new equipment is bought so that labor costs can be reduced, products and markets change, and so on. Many of these changes may require modifications in the gainsharing formula. Such obvious changes as new capital, new equipment, and changes in product mix should be anticipated in advance so that they can be handled relatively automatically by established rules and procedures. The need for more serious change should also be anticipated, and a formal process for altering the formula and changing the plan should be formulated at the beginning.

This is usually done by establishing a group that is responsible for the management and fine-tuning of the plan. In practice, this group often evolves from the group that put the plan together. It is important that this group have the same high credibility as the design group and that it represent a good cross-section of the organization. If it does not, the changes are likely to be seen as efforts on the part of management to subvert the plan or stop payouts from occurring. The recommendation, then, is that a steering committee be appointed to handle unanticipated changes and be responsible for regularly updating the plan.

Organizations often lack the ability to credibly modify the design of their gainsharing plan in ways that are trusted by the vast majority of the employees. This is not a problem as long as things are stable, but it becomes a big one as soon as a major change occurs and an alteration in the formula is needed. For example, I was recently asked to consult with a chemical company that had problems with its gainsharing plan. It had worked well for about a year but then they changed products. Suddenly their formula called for large bonus checks (over 40 percent of base salary) even though all agreed they were not justified. The problem was that a new product needed less labor and that the formula was not changed to reflect it. The consultant who installed the plan had used a packaged approach and had not taught the people in the organization how to modify the plan. He had simply told them, "Here is the plan. I will show you how to run it." As a result the organization had administrative skills, but not design skills.

The Participative System

An essential part of gainsharing plans is the participative system. Not all gainsharing plans include participative systems. For example, many early installations of the Improshare Plan did not include participative-management systems. Today, most gainsharing plans include some form of participative management. Mitchell Fein, the creator of the Improshare Plan, now recommends combining it with quality circles.

In most cases, a participative system is needed in order for gainsharing to work; and in virtually every case, it is needed in order for the potential of the plan to be realized. In the absence of a change in employee behavior, there is no reason to expect a payout from the typical gainsharing plan. A payout requires an improvement in performance, which, in turn, requires more effective behavior on the part of employees. Simply changing rewards often is not enough given the poor line of sight that exists in most gainsharing plans; information, knowledge, and power also need to be affected.

Tying pay to performance may improve employee motivation if the line of sight is good, especially in small organizations. It also may work in situations where the work is not highly skilled or interdependent and, as a result, effort is directly related to performance. In most situations, however, there are several reasons why a gainsharing plan without a participative system should not be expected to appreciably improve performance or increase bonuses.

First of all, the motivational impact may be small. Most gainsharing plans aggregate a number of people together; as a result, the perceived relationship between individual performance and individual pay increases only slightly. In addition, simple effort and good intentions are not enough to improve the operating results of many organizations. What is needed is a combination of efforts to work harder, work more effectively together, share ideas, and work "smarter." This, in turn, often takes a formal participative system that harnesses the willingness of people to offer their ideas and turns this willingness into actual changes in operating procedures and systems. In the absence of some form of participative management, these changes rarely seem to occur.

In participative gainsharing plans, such as the Scanlon and the Rucker plans, the key participative structure is a formal suggestion system with written suggestions and shop-floor committees to review the suggestions. There is also a higher-level review committee that reviews these recommendations if major changes are called for. This committee usually draws its membership from several parts of the organization. This system of committees is one way of trying to assure that new ideas will be seriously considered and, where appropriate, implemented.

In many ways, this committee structure resembles the parallel-structure approach used by quality circles and by QWL programs. The differences are that they start with written suggestions, often have a small budget to implement suggestions, and can decide to implement ideas that affect their work areas. Thus, in several respects, they are more participative than quality circles. They are also older and an American invention. Given this, it is surprising that American managers have focused on quality circles and Japan in order to learn about participative-suggestion programs. They might learn more by focusing on Michigan and what Donnelly Mirrors has been doing for decades, although trips to Holland, Michigan, fall a bit short of trips to Japan!

As with quality circles, it is not easy to get participative committees effectively operating in most gainsharing organizations. Many individuals do not have the skills to operate effectively in this kind of participative environment. In addition, managers are sometimes resistant to having committees of workers participate more actively in workplace decision making because they see their roles being undermined.

Conditions Favoring Gainsharing

Not all situations are right for the installation of a gainsharing plan. Table 3 highlights conditions that favor gainsharing. The reasons why most of these conditions favor a gain-

Table 3. Conditions Favoring Gainsharing Plans.

Organizational Characteristic	Favorable Condition
Size	Small unit, usually less than 500 employees
Age	Old enough so that learning curve has flattened and standards can be set based on performance history
Financial measures	Simple, with a good history
Market for output	Good, can absorb additional production
Product costs	Controllable by employees
Organizational climate	Open, high level of trust
Style of management	Participative
Union status	No union, or one that is favorable to a cooperative effort
Overtime history	Limited to no use of overtime in past
Seasonal nature of business	Relatively stable across time
Workfloor interdependence	High to moderate interdependence
Capital investment plans	Little investment planned
Product stability	Few product changes
Comptroller or chief financial officer	Trusted, able to explain financial measures
Communication policy	Open, willing to share financial results
Plant manager	Trust, committed to plan, able to articulate goals and ideals of plan
Management	Technically competent, supportive of participative management style, good communications skills, able to deal with suggestions and new ideas
Corporate position (if part of large organization)	Favorable to plan
Work force	Technically knowledgeable, interested in participation and higher pay, financially knowledgeable or interested
Plant support services	Maintenance and engineering groups competent, willing, and able to respond to increased demands.

sharing plan are self-evident. However, in some cases they are not obvious and thus a brief review of them follows (Lawler, 1981).

- *Market.* The plan should lead to increased productivity. If the market cannot absorb this, it can lead to a need for lay-offs and can undermine the plan.
- *Overtime History.* A history of high amounts of overtime hours can cause problems if individuals have become dependent on overtime pay. The plan can cause increased productivity and, as a result, less overtime and less total pay. This can cause employees to set quotas and to restrict their productivity.
- *Seasonal Nature.* Organizations that have a seasonal business often have to hire and lay off people on a month-to-month basis. This can undermine the plan's promotion of group awareness and lead to restriction of production during slow seasons.
- *Financial Officer.* Most plans require a spokesperson who is articulate and trusted in order for individuals to see the pay-performance relationship. The financial officer is in an ideal position to do this.
- *Capital Investment and Product Stability.* It is easier to compute a bonus when there are no changes in equipment or product.
- *Support Service Group.* As with quality circles, the installation of a plan often brings requests from employees for changes that will help them do their work more effectively. These must be responded to effectively or discouragement is likely to set in.
- *Management.* It is impossible to overemphasize the importance of management to the success of gainsharing. Because it is a participative-management approach it needs leadership, vision, and supportive behavior from the managers. All too often these are not present. Gainsharing puts particular pressure on the first-level supervisors. They are expected to change their behavior and, unfortunately, often do not. As many as 50 percent of the first-level supervisors in many

plants cannot adapt. The kind of management attitude that kills gainsharing is illustrated by the following memo from an engineering manager at a company that recently instituted gainsharing.

> My best judgment of John's contribution to this business places his gainsharing analysis work as the "least productive" use of his time.
>
> Employee suggestions, as motivated by our system, cannot be expected to have a high meritorious content. Generally, they are generated by an untrained, unskilled author with a myopic viewpoint and little understanding of business ramifications. Our hope is, I presume, that the author's closeness to a specific problem may occasionally provide a thought that has been overlooked that can provide true return on investment. The chaff-to-wheat ratio in all suggestion programs is high and especially so when suggestions are solicited by volume rather than content.
>
> This is not to express that Engineering does not support our gainsharing program. We fully recognize the merit of involving employees in their work and the employee-relations benefits attendant thereto.

Top management is also crucial. I once worked with a plant manager who personally killed a plan. He continuously referred to it as the "employee bribe plan" and resisted every suggestion. Just the opposite is needed if gainsharing is to work. Positive leadership is clearly present at Motorola, where gainsharing has been made a major corporate theme, and at Dana Corporation, where top management has given it strong support (O'Toole, 1985).

In no situation are all of the favorable conditions listed in Table 3 likely to be present. If they were, a gainsharing plan probably would be easy to install, but, if it were installed, relatively little gain would be expected. In one plant I worked with, almost all the conditions were met. As expected, it was relatively easy to install the plan. Gains were realized quickly but they were modest simply because the plant was already working quite effectively.

Most plans start with suboptimal conditions. A plan may work in conditions that are not favorable at first but are changed after the plan is installed. The challenge in deciding whether to install a plan is to analyze the situation in terms of what conditions are favorable, what conditions are unfavorable and unchangeable, and what conditions are unfavorable but changeable. The next step is to decide whether or not it is worth trying a plan. Unfortunately, no formulas or rules exist to indicate how these conditions should be combined to make a decision. It seems, however, that if a majority of the existing conditions are unfavorable, it is probably not worth going ahead with a plan installation. Finally, it is clear that if the union is disapproving and the measures are inadequate, there is no sense in pursuing a plan, regardless of whether the other conditions are favorable.

Despite the conservative flavor of the last paragraph, I have often found that with gainsharing, where there is a will there is usually a way. In other words, gainsharing can work even though the situation is not favorable if extra work is done. This is perhaps most clearly demonstrated by Motorola. Many of the conditions there were not right, but they wanted gainsharing to be part of their participative-management approach, so they are finding a way to make it work.

The Scanlon Plan

The Scanlon Plan is undoubtedly the best-known gainsharing plan. It was developed by Joe Scanlon, a union leader, in the 1930s. In this plan, bonuses based on a measure of company or plant performance are given to all employees. As was mentioned earlier, the plan focuses on labor costs relative to productivity.

Proponents of the plan argue that it should not be regarded as just another incentive plan. To quote from two of his followers, Lesieur and Puckett (1969):

> Scanlon deeply believed that the typical organization did not elicit the full potential from employees, either as individuals or as a group. He did not feel that the commonly held concept that "the boss is the boss and a worker works" was a proper basis for stimulating the interest of employees in company problems; rather, he felt such a concept reinforced employees' beliefs that there was an "enemy" somewhere above them in the hierarchy and that a cautious suspicion should be maintained at all times. He felt that employee interest and contribution could best be stimulated by providing the employee with a maximum amount of information and data concerning company problems and successes, and by soliciting his contribution as to how he felt the problem might best be solved and the job best done. Thus, the Scanlon Plan is a common sharing between management and employees of problems, goals, and ideas.

Scanlon realized that if his management philosophy was to be implemented, some structural changes were needed in organizations. He pointed out that most wage systems fail to reward individuals for cooperative behavior and fail to produce a convergence between the goals of employees and the goals of the organization. (This sounds strikingly similar to what was said earlier about moving rewards, power, information, and knowledge downward.) Scanlon also believed that the opinions and ideas of people lower down in organizations are ignored, even though they are of value. To correct this situation, he suggested that organizations use a suggestion system. (This may sound like the thinking behind quality circles but Scanlon was decades earlier!).

The genius of the Scanlon Plan, and of Joe Scanlon, is the recognition that a commitment to participation and joint problem solving is not enough. Effective use of participatory management requires a congruence between the pay system of an organization and its other features. Joe Scanlon was one of the first to articulate the influence of the fit between pay systems and management philosophy on an organization. The pay system is an important part of the Scanlon approach to management because it ties the goals of individuals to the goals of the organization. When the pay system is operating properly, the better the organization functions, the better off the employees are. It is therefore to the advantage of employees to produce more, to work faster and more effectively, to cooperate with other employees, to adopt new technologies, and to make suggestions that improve organizational effectiveness.

The Scanlon Plan has been around long enough to allow some conclusions to be drawn about its effectiveness. The conclusions must be tentative, however, because little actual research has been done on the plan, and most of what has been done is of low quality. Estimates vary on how many firms have tried the plan; before 1970, the figure is thought to be less than five hundred. Interest in the plan has increased tremendously since 1970 and, as a result, there are many more Scanlon Plans. Traditionally, most Scanlon Plans have covered whole companies, usually small, privately owned companies. Recently, some large organizations have successfully implemented the plan on a plant-by-plant basis. This has resulted in some companies (such as the Dana Corporation) having as many as twenty different plans. If this approach is adopted by other companies, it could dramatically increase the number of plans that are in existence.

A review of the literature on Scanlon Plans found studies covering fifty-three situations where the plan was tried (Bullock and Lawler, 1984). This is a rather large number of cases. Unfortunately, the data from most of these cases are poor, and it is therefore difficult to determine just what impact the plan has had in most situations. It is possible, however, to code forty-four of the cases in terms of whether the plan was successful in contributing to organizational effectiveness. The apparent successes outnumber the failures by thirty to fourteen. This is an impressive success rate, but it may be inflated because organizations that are successful in introducing the plan are more likely to write about their experiences. Similarly, researchers are more likely to report positive results than negative ones. However, even if we discount the two-to-one success-to-failure ratio because of reporting bias, the success ratio is still impressive and probably indicates that Scanlon Plans are successful at least half the time. The following are likely outcomes when the plan is successful.

1. Coordination, teamwork, and sharing of knowledge at lower levels are enhanced.
2. Social needs are recognized through participation and mutually reinforcing group behavior.
3. Attention is focused on cost savings, not just quantity of production.
4. Acceptance of change due to technology, market, and new methods is greater because higher efficiency leads to bonuses.
5. Attitudinal change occurs among workers, and they demand more efficient management and better planning.
6. Workers try to reduce overtime and to work smarter, not harder or faster.
7. Workers produce ideas as well as effort.
8. More flexible administration of union-management relations occurs.
9. If present, the union is strengthened because it is responsible for a better work situation and higher pay.

It is interesting to note that higher employee satisfaction and a better quality of work life are not among the outcomes listed. The reason for this is that few studies have looked at the impact of the Scanlon Plan on the quality of work life. There is some evidence, however, that it does have a positive impact. First, it leads to higher pay because of the bonus and this increases satisfaction. Second, the outcomes listed often contribute to employee satisfaction. Third, several studies, including one by myself at Donnelly Mirrors, have found high satisfaction and commitment levels in Scanlon companies.

Research has identified a number of reasons why Scanlon Plans may fail. Some of these are due to poor implementation of a potentially good plan. Others are due to more basic flaws that limit the plan's effectiveness in a number of situations. The following are the most frequent reasons plans fail.

- *Formula Construction.* The formula needs to accurately measure conditions in the organization and must be adjustable as they change. Often, rigid formulas that do not reflect employee behavior lead to failure.
- *Payout Level.* It is important that some bonuses be paid, particularly at the beginning. Sometimes this does not happen because the performance level that must be achieved before a bonus is paid is set too high.
- *Management Attitudes.* Unless managers are favorable to the idea of participation, the plan will not fit the management style of the organization. In some organizations, the plan has been tried simply as a pay incentive without regard to the management style, and it has failed because of a poor fit.
- *Plan Focus.* Many plans focus only on labor savings. This presents problems in organizations where other costs are great and are under the control of the employees. It can lead to the other costs being ignored or even increased in order to reduce labor costs.
- *Communication.* For the plan to work, employees must understand and trust it enough to believe that their pay will increase if they perform better. For this belief to occur, a great deal of open communication and education is needed. Often this is ignored and, as a result, plans fail.
- *Union Cooperation.* For the Scanlon Plan to succeed, the local union must be supportive. In most of the places where it has been tried, the local union has supported it. However, some failures have occurred in situations where unions have not supported it sufficiently.
- *Threat to Supervisor.* The plan changes the roles of supervisors. They are forced to deal with many suggestions, and their competence is tested and questioned in new ways. Unless supervisors are prepared to accept these changes, the plan can fail.

In summary, there is evidence that the introduction of a Scanlon Plan can lead to a higher quality of work life and greater organizational effectiveness. However, the evidence clearly shows that for a variety of reasons these benefits are not always obtained when Scanlon Plans are introduced.

The Rucker Plan

The Rucker Plan was developed by Allen Rucker of the Eddy-Rucker-Nichols consulting firm, which has specialized in this plan for over thirty-five years. Under the Rucker Plan, a historical relationship is established between the total earnings of hourly employees and the production value created by the company or plant. According to one proponent of the plan, this relationship will be stable in ninety-five out of one hundred manufacturing firms and can be used as a basis for sharing production gains. Production value is equivalent to the value added by the manufacturer; that is, sales income less material and supply costs. As in the Scanlon Plan, a historical base period and a ratio are used. When improvement takes place, a bonus pool is generated and it is split between the employees and the company.

There is very little evidence available on the effectiveness of the Rucker Plan, making it impossible to make any statement about its usual success rate. In many ways, the Rucker Plan is similar to the Scanlon Plan and, as such, might be expected to have a similar success rate. However, it differs in some important aspects. It takes a different approach to measurement so that changes in material costs will affect the bonus. It also places less emphasis on building a participative-management system. Descriptions of the Rucker Plan mention problem-solving groups, but they do not seem to be as central as they are to the Scanlon Plan. There is, however, no reason why an organization that wants to install the plan could not place a strong emphasis on participation.

The plan adds an alternative computational formula that, in some situations, may be better than the one typically used in the Scanlon Plan. As such, it can be used as a good basis for a participative gainsharing plan. It is particularly applicable to manufacturing situations and especially where it is important to include material and other costs in the plan. One note of caution is in order: it is based on a complex formula and as such needs considerable education and training.

Improshare

An industrial engineer, Mitchell Fein, has developed a gainsharing plan that is based on many of the same measures as are individual incentive plans. The plan, Improshare, can be applied at either the plant or group level. Unlike the Scanlon Plan, it is based on engineered performance standards. Like the Scanlon Plan, it uses a historical standard, covers everyone, and measures only labor costs. Improshare plans use a formula that looks at the ratio of units produced to hours worked. A bonus is paid when more units are produced per hours worked—in other words, when productivity increases. It also includes a buy-back provision that allows management to change the standard in return for a one-time bonus payment. The buy-back is intended to be used in case of technological or organizational change.

Improshare was first installed in organizations during the middle 1970s. At that time, it was not particularly associated with a participative approach to management; rather, it was associated with a more traditional approach. Recently, this situation has changed considerably. The Improshare Plan is now frequently installed in conjunction with a quality-circle program in order to put in place some of the participative-management principles that are so characteristic of the Scanlon Plan.

No exact numbers are available, but a good estimate is that at least 150 organizations have adopted the Improshare Plan and there are a number of success stories in the popular press. Fein talks of productivity gains of 25 percent with bigger gains possible when quality circles are used in conjunction with it.

In many respects, the future looks bright for this type of plan. It combines a moderate to low level of participation with a relatively simple financial formula. The simplicity of the formula is its greatest strength and its greatest weakness. It often turns out that the formula is too simple and needs to be revised to more accurately reflect the situation in an organization. In particular, it may need to include other costs. Nevertheless, the formula provides a starting point for other more complicated measures, just as does the simple Scanlon Plan labor-only formula. Similarly, the quality-circle programs that are often combined with it represent a start toward participative management, although, as we stressed earlier, they represent a small step.

Profit Sharing

Many employees are covered by profit-sharing plans. According to one study, over 350,000 firms in the United States have some form of profit sharing. Most of the profit-sharing plans (about 75 percent, according to one estimate) defer the payment until retirement and, as such, are not true incentive plans (Metzger, 1975). Many others combine a partial payout with deferment. Thus, in only a few cases (often in smaller companies) is profit sharing used as an incentive. In most organizations, profits are so far beyond the direct influence of most employees that profit-based bonuses are simply not likely to be effective motivators. The exception would seem to be the smaller organization in which labor costs are a very high proportion of all costs. In this situation, a bonus based on profits may act as a motivator. Finally, although some organizations combine their profit-sharing plan with a participative style of management, most do not.

Hewlett Packard tries to use its organization-wide profit-sharing plan as a true incentive and reinforcer of participative management. Its effectiveness, however, is limited because of the large number of employees in the corporation and the resulting weak connection or line of sight from individual performance to the profit-sharing bonus. People Express, the very successful new airline, has also used profit sharing as an incentive and reinforcer of participative management. It worked well when the organization was small but has lost part of its effectiveness as the organization has grown. As a result, it is now combined with gainsharing plans that provide a better line of sight.

Overall, profit sharing has limited usefulness as a motivator. The exception is in very small organizations, where it can be used as a measurement approach that has some line of sight. Occasionally, a larger organization can make good use of profit sharing as part of its overall philosophy of management. Hewlett Packard, for example, uses it as a vehicle for communicating to employees how the company is doing. It can also play a role in establishing a positive organization culture. It can help reinforce the fact that everyone stands to gain from performance improvement and that everyone is part of the same organization. Traditional profit-sharing companies, such as Kodak and Sears, have used their profit-sharing plans in this way for decades. General Motors and Ford have recently added it, partly as a result of concessionary bargaining and partly as a way of impressing upon employees that people are critical to the long-term success of their organizations.

Impact on Rewards, Information, Knowledge, and Power

Gainsharing plans differ in some important ways from the participative plans that have been reviewed so far. First, they are the only approach that moves financial rewards based on organizational performance down in the organization. This has important implications for motivation as well as for the long-term viability of the program. In those organizations where payouts have occurred, gainsharing has quickly become institutionalized and has, in some companies, survived for decades.

When gainsharing is combined with a participative-management philosophy, it also typically moves operating information downward in the organization. Because payouts are linked to financial results, there is strong pressure to share financial data with employees. This serves to empower them and increases the chance that participation will be effective.

Although gainsharing moves some power downward in

organizations, its effect in this area is limited. Power moves downward partially because information moves downward. Power also moves downward to the degree that groups are allowed to have a budget and implement solutions. However, because the approach does not directly change work or organization structure, power does not dramatically move downward. Like quality circles, gainsharing can best be described as a parallel-structure approach to participation. In my experience, it is a more powerful force for changes in power than quality circles are. Because employees receive financial information and their pay depends on effectiveness, they will challenge managers and demand change in ways that do not occur with quality circles. For example, I have seen employees ask vice-presidents about accounts receivable and marketing issues.

Gainsharing can have some effect on the knowledge and skills of the work force. The impact here is very similar to that of quality circles except that, in addition to problem-solving and group-process skill, gainsharing plans usually increase employee knowledge about the economics of the business.

It is important to mention one last strength of gainsharing plans: they affect everyone—there is no danger of a small group being affected while others are left out. In addition, because everyone is affected, the chances are good for an immediate significant improvement in organizational effectiveness.

Effectiveness of Gainsharing

There is enough experience with gainsharing plans to clearly establish that they can improve organizational effectiveness through increasing employee involvement. The positive results of gainsharing plans are summarized in the list below.

- Work methods and procedures improve through suggestion program.
- Attraction and retention improve because of higher pay and more participation.
- Quality improves because of motivation and better methods.
- Rate of output improves due to motivation and better methods.

- Decision making may improve because of suggestion program and more knowledge.
- Skills of employees may increase in financial decision-making and group-process areas.

Staffing flexibility and grievances are not directly affected by gainsharing plans. There is no reduction in staff support or supervision. The reason for the many positive results is obvious. Gainsharing increases people's psychological and financial stake in the business—two important motivators.

A good example of what can be accomplished with gainsharing is a plan that was participatively developed for a plant that is part of a *Fortune* 500 company (Bullock and Bullock, 1982). The formula that was developed by R. J. Bullock and myself used a historical base and measured the cost per ton of product produced. It focused on such controllable costs as salaries, benefits, rework, and materials. During the first year, significant improvements occurred. Tons per labor hour increased 27.2 percent, scrap rate improved 14.3 percent, and there was a 64.2 percent net margin improvement. These financial improvements are even more impressive because the plant was one of the most profitable in the corporation before the plan was installed.

A good idea of how these gains were accomplished can be obtained from looking at before and after survey data and suggestion-system results. The average employee produced just less than one suggestion and the acceptance rate was 79 percent, for a net savings per employee of $441.16. Attitudes improved in all areas, including openness, communications, and teamwork.

Although the results from this gainsharing plan are unusually positive, there are many other examples of success. Eggers Industries installed a Scanlon Plan in their Two Rivers, Wisconsin, plywood plant. In its first two years it produced a 26 percent reduction in labor costs (Dulworth, 1985). Nucor Steel has used gainsharing as part of its strategy for competing with offshore producers of steel. It produces steel for $60 a ton, which is close to the Japanese cost and about half that for other U.S. producers.

Some of the expected negative consequences of the plans

are listed below. These negative consequences come from the fact that the participative systems generally associated with gainsharing plans are, in fact, parallel structures. That is, they involve quality-circle meetings or Scanlon Plan problem-solving meetings that typically are outside the normal organizational structure. As such, they have many of the disadvantages that quality-circle programs have. Nevertheless, they are likely to be more successful since they combine financial participation and problem solving. They affect another very important part of an organization, the pay system, and they do something to cause information to be shared broadly in the organization. They also can be used in unionized locations since many unions favor them.

- Salary costs will go up.
- Training costs will go up.
- Support personnel will increase because the plans require administrators.
- Unmet expectations for organizational change may exist.
- Resistance by middle management will increase because suggestions will affect them.
- Resistance by staff support groups will increase because suggestions will affect them.
- Unmet expectations for personal growth and development may exist because of limited form of participation.
- Time is spent in meetings, and decisions can be slow.

The problem with the existing plans is that they do not fit well in all situations. So far, few have been tried in service- and knowledge-oriented work situations. It is extremely important that they be developed for these situations, since more and more work is of this nature. Failure to develop gainsharing plans for these settings can seriously limit the effectiveness of participative-management programs in nonmanufacturing settings. Gainsharing plans need to be a key component of almost all high-involvement management systems. It is hard to imagine a long-term successful participative venture in which financial participation is not part of the overall effort. Thus, plans need to be developed that will fit all types of organizations.

In conclusion, the best way to view such traditional gain-sharing plans as the Scanlon Plan is as a possible first step toward high-involvement management. They institute a low-level participative process and a bonus formula. This contribution has the possibility of leading to other changes in the organization. The bonus can be a powerful force toward changes in other features of the organization because it rewards improvements in performance. The initial experience with a parallel-organization participative approach, if successful, can set the stage for more significant changes in power, information, and knowledge.

❧❧❧ 10

New-Design Plants

❧❧❧❧❧❧❧❧❧❧

A not-so-quiet revolution has occurred in a number of major U.S. corporations over the past decade. They have designed, built, and managed one or more new plants that are revolutionary in the degree to which they move power, information, intrinsic rewards, and knowledge downward (Lawler, 1978).

The list of companies with new-design plants reads like a who's who of the *Fortune* 500. They include AT&T, General Foods, PPG Industries, Procter & Gamble, Sherwin-Williams, TRW, H. J. Heinz, Rockwell, Johnson and Johnson, General Motors, Mead, and Cummins Engine. Many of these organizations have started not one high-involvement plant, but two, three, four, or more. At this point, no one knows precisely how many organizations have initiated new-design plants, nor how many of them exist. A good guess would be that at least forty large corporations have one or more, and that, overall, two hundred or more are in operation (Walton, 1985).

The development of new-design plants in the United States began with those started by Procter & Gamble. During the early 1970s, its paper division made a substantial commitment to participative management by introducing it in several new plants. The participative approach that guided them had its major origins in Europe. It is often called the sociotechnical approach. It emphasizes fitting together the social and technical systems in organizations to allow for participative management. As was mentioned earlier in our discussion of teams, the pioneering research and theory was developed in Norway and England. Today there are more than twenty participative new-design plants in Procter & Gamble.

The participative model used by Procter & Gamble first spread to General Foods' highly publicized Topeka, Kansas, Gaines dog food plant. This plant became famous and was copied by a number of other companies. Procter & Gamble, however, has maintained a closed-door policy with respect to their new plants and, as a result, has received much less publicity. Many of the individuals who worked on the design of the new Procter & Gamble plants have become consultants and have gone to other companies. This, along with the work of other consultants, has spread expertise in new-design plants to many companies.

New-design plants do a great deal to move power, information, and knowledge to the lowest levels of an organization. Although they are not complete participative systems, in many respects they represent the best example in the United States of a congruent organization-wide approach to participative management. Most of their systems are oriented toward participative management. More than any approach that has been reviewed so far, they represent an organizational design that is consistent with the idea of moving power, information, knowledge, and rewards to the lowest levels.

Characteristics of the New-Design Plants

One of the most interesting aspects of new-design plants is the number of participative practices common to all or almost all of them. A review of these will indicate just how specific areas of management have been affected and how these plants differ from traditional plants.

Employee Selection. The traditional approach to employee selection is eliminated. Instead of the personnel department carefully screening, testing, and selecting applicants, a process is used that includes helping the job applicant make a valid decision about taking the job and getting production employees involved in selecting their co-workers. The selection process places a great deal of emphasis on acquainting people with the nature of the jobs they are expected to fill and the nature of the managerial style that will be used in the plant. They can then decide whether the situation is right for them.

The hiring process uses a group interview, which is initially conducted by the start-up design team. Potential employees are questioned about their attitudes toward participation and their interpersonal skills are observed to determine whether the job applicant will fit this management approach. After the plant becomes operational, production employees are given the responsibility for selecting new members of their teams.

Design of the Physical Layout. Many of the high-involvement plants make an effort to have at least a few members of the work force on board early enough to participate in decisions about the layout of machinery, equipment, and the recreational and personal areas of the plant. The idea is to capture the employees' ideas in order to improve the design of the plant. Often employees from existing plants—many of whom will be reassigned to the new plant—are asked to participate in the design. In some cases, experts in sociotechnical system design are also called in to make certain that the physical layout is congruent with the desired social system.

The computer manufacturing example mentioned in an earlier chapter underlines just how important it is to get all parties involved early in the design process. In that situation, the management team developed a team-based approach to the manufacture of personal computers. Just as it finished its design, it discovered that the corporate engineering department had ordered equipment for an assembly line.

The principles of sociotechnical design typically lead to work configurations that support the team concept. The plant is laid out so that work teams have their own areas and so that members of the team can easily see and communicate with each other. Typically, breaks in the work flow are put before and after the work done by a team so that the team can get a sense of doing a whole piece of work and, of course, the organization can hold the team accountable for doing an entire piece of work. Team meeting rooms are also often provided so that when a work problem comes up or a discussion is needed, it is relatively easy for the teams to meet. The Volvo plant at Kalmar is a prime example of this type of design. There, teams not only have responsibility for putting together entire systems in a car (such as the electrical system), they have their own work area entrances and personal facilities. The General Motors' Saturn project uses this approach, as well.

Frequently, a strong egalitarian emphasis exists. Rather than having separate areas in which managers eat and spend their nonwork time, everyone uses the same eating, restroom, and recreational facilities. In many plants, the entrances and parking areas are common to all employees. In other words, employees all receive a clear message that at least in terms of the physical facilities and the typical perquisites of office, an egalitarian system exists. According to the following report in the *Wall Street Journal* (Aug. 2, 1985, p. 1) General Motors plans on using this approach in their new Saturn office building.

At General Motors Corp's new Saturn headquarters in Troy, Mich., everybody will be equal. But the office design firm GM hired to furnish the new building didn't quite believe that.

Saturn managers told the firm, which GM won't name, that the furniture and carpeting in every office had to be exactly the same grade and quality—no special treatment for the executives. But the design company ordered special furniture and decorations for Saturn's eight top officials anyway. "More expensive desks, credenzas, lamps, ashtrays, the whole shot," says a GM employee.

Saturn officials stuck to their principles: They canceled that part of the order. Not taking the "executive" furniture saved the company more than $1 million.

Job Design. In all the plants, an attempt is made to see that employees have jobs that are challenging, motivating, and satisfying. In a few cases, this is done through individually based job-enrichment approaches that emphasize personal responsibility for a whole piece of meaningful work. In most cases, however, it is accomplished through the creation of teams.

As was discussed earlier, teams are given the responsibility for the production of a whole product. They are self-managing in the sense that they make decisions about who performs which tasks on a given day. They set their own production goals and are often also responsible for quality control, purchasing, and the control of absenteeism. Most teams emphasize the desirability of job rotation for their members. Team members are expected to learn all the jobs that fall within the purview of the group.

In some plants, an effort is made to mix interesting tasks with routine ones. For example, one plant made the maintenance jobs part of the same team as warehousing so that no one spends all of his or her time on the relatively boring aspects of warehousing. The end result of using work teams is usually that the participants feel responsible for a large work area, experience a sense of control, and develop an understanding for a large segment of the production process.

Pay System. In order to reinforce the egalitarian climate and culture in an organization, all employees are placed on salary. This means that time clocks and the traditional distinctions associated with being an hourly employee are dropped. In many cases, identical fringe-benefit packages are given to all employees. Of course, overtime records still must be kept for non-exempt employees because of federal law. This is usually handled by an employee simply turning in a time sheet that reports the number of overtime hours worked.

Most new plants have taken a skill-based approach to establishing pay levels for employees. Instead of using a job evaluation approach, they evaluate the skills of each individual (Lawler and Ledford, 1985). Typically, everyone starts at the same salary. As new skills are learned, the salary goes up. When this system is combined with job rotation, a person doing a relatively low-level job may be quite highly paid because he or she is capable of performing a large number of tasks.

This approach has two main advantages. It tends to create a flexible, highly trained work force, and it avoids the problems associated with maintaining pay rates for many different jobs. It also promotes the development of the work team because for the team to work effectively, its members must know more than one job. Basing pay on the number of skills mastered obviously encourages people to expand their skills.

In many of the new-design plants, decisions about whether or not an individual has mastered a new skill well enough to deserve a salary increase are left to the members of his or her team. This approach to pay decisions reinforces the participative-management style because it asks employees to make a very important decision.

A few new-design plants have moved toward plant-wide profit-sharing or gainsharing plans. It is possible that as the rest of them mature and establish stable base periods for the measurement of productivity gains, more of them will adopt these plans. Organization-wide sharing of productivity gains is congruent with the team concept of management and the general participative egalitarian principles that underlie the design of these plants. In several instances, I have installed gainsharing plans after plants have matured somewhat (after three to seven years) and the effects have been quite positive. It represents a useful way to overcome the "topping out" problem (to be discussed later) that new-design plants often suffer.

Organizational Structure. One of the really striking innovations in most new-design plants is the lack of hierarchy. All the plants have placed the plant manager only a few management levels above the production workers. In some cases, the foreman's role has been eliminated completely. In others, the foremen report directly to the plant manager and such traditional intermediate levels as general foreman and superintendent have been eliminated.

Where there are no foremen, several teams usually report to a single supervisor or area manager. Most of the time, the teams elect a team leader who is responsible for communicating with the rest of the organization. This person undertakes the lateral relations with other functional and line departments that consume so much time and constitute such an important responsibility for the typical first-line supervisor. This leads to situations where the number of managers can be reduced to one for every hundred employees, as it is in a General Motors' Delco plant. It also allows a Scott Paper Company plant to operate during off-shifts without any management personnel being present.

New-design plants also de-emphasize functional responsibility. Rather than being organized on a functional basis (maintenance, production, and so on), they tend to be organized on a product or an area basis. Thus, individuals have the responsibility for the production of a product rather than for general maintenance or engineering. This system provides more meaningful job structures and creates a feeling of commitment to the product rather than to a function.

The new-design plants also tend to be very lightly staffed in support personnel (such as scheduling, engineering, and quality control). It is common to find reductions of as much as 30 percent in this area. Many of the functions typically done by staff support groups are done by work teams. For example, since scheduling, certain kinds of record keeping, and even some purchasing decisions are made in work teams, there does not need to be as much staff support available in these areas. Because of the reduced need for staff, plants can operate like the General Motors' Delco plant mentioned earlier, with just over 20 white-collar employees for over 400 production employees.

The roles of staff support specialists are often quite different than they are in traditional plants. Since the new plants place most decisions in work teams, employees in staff jobs become consultants to and trainers of the production teams rather than decision makers. This requires a very different type of person and, as a result, often causes stress in the staff support areas.

Approach to Training. New-design plants place heavy emphasis on training, career planning, and the personal development of employees. This is usually backed up with extensive in-plant training programs and strong encouragement for employees to take off-the-job training, usually paid for by the organization.

There have been some interesting innovations in training. For example, in some plants, employees take courses in the economics of the plant's business and are rewarded with higher pay when they complete the courses. On-the-job training by peers is also very common and is necessary to implement the concept of multi-skilled employees. Regular career-planning sessions are also scheduled. In some plants, employees present a personal career-development plan to their team members; in others, the process is handled by someone in management. As a result of the strong emphasis on training, workers develop the feeling that personal development and growth are desirable goals and it becomes an important part of the culture.

Management Philosophy. Many new-design plants have written management philosophy statements. These usually include the values that are important to the management of the plant and always include statements about how people should and will be treated in the organization. These vary in length from a few lines to several pages. They are not meant to be detailed operating statements. Rather, they are meant to express the culture and values. They typically form a type of touchstone for the organization that can be reviewed as the plant matures. They also are used as a check to be sure that new developments are congruent with the original philosophy. They are very important documents and are widely distributed and displayed.

A good example of a philosophy that was developed jointly with a union is the following agreement between Shell Canada and the Energy and Chemical Workers Union in 1981.

Employees are responsible and trustworthy, capable of working together effectively and making proper decisions related to their spheres of responsibilities and work arrangement—if given the necessary authorities, information and training.

Employees should be permitted to contribute and grow to their fullest capability and potential without constraints or artificial barriers, with compensation based on their demonstrated knowledge and skills rather than on tasks being performed at any specific time.

To achieve the most effective overall results, it is deemed necessary that a climate exists which will encourage initiative, experimentation and generation of new ideas, supported by an open and meaningful two-way communication system.

New-Design Plants and Participation

New-design plants are particularly effective in moving power, information, and knowledge to lower levels. The combination of cross-training, group-skills training, and economic education does a great deal to move knowledge to lower levels. Most plants report on operating results and have open information systems, so that a good deal of information is shared downward. However, no structure is built into the model to assure this, so it can be an area of weakness.

Probably the greatest weakness is in the area of rewards. The absence of gainsharing, profit sharing, and stock ownership means that rewards are not necessarily shared downward in the organization. This weakness may be a major cause of the mid-life crisis that these plants seem to encounter. Because there is no direct financial involvement in the business, it is often difficult for employees to keep striving for higher levels of performance. Nevertheless, given our earlier discussion of what establishes an effective participative system, we would predict that new-design plants should be quite successful. More than any other approach discussed so far, they move power, information, and knowledge downward.

Overall, new design plants are clearly different from traditional plants in a number of important ways. Almost no aspect of the organization is left untouched. The reward system, the structure, the physical layout, the personnel management system, and the nature of jobs are all changed in significant ways. Because so many features are altered, in aggregate they amount to a new kind of organization.

I must stress, however, that most new-design plants are still regarded by both employees and management as being in an evolutionary stage. They are being modified and altered continually on the basis of experience. Thus, although it is clear that a common set of innovations is being tried, every plant and organization is simultaneously adapting them in ways that make the management system and overall design of each unique.

Effectiveness of New-Design Plants

There are almost no hard data on how economically effective new-design plants are. In a few cases, the plants have been measured by outsiders, who report positive results. For example, the Topeka plant of General Foods has been studied by Richard Walton, as well as by Douglas Jenkins and myself. Both studies reported low absenteeism, low turnover, low production costs, high quality, and high employee satisfaction. Similarly, an internal study estimated that production costs were as much as 40 percent lower than those of a comparable traditionally managed General Foods plant.

Unfortunately, the Topeka plant is the exception as far as public data on organizational effectiveness are concerned. Comparable data simply are not available on most other new-design plants.

Some interesting data are available on an AT&T new-design start-up. AT&T created a new organization, American Transtech, to handle the paperwork associated with stockholder relations. With the new organization, they report being able to handle a 600 percent increase in accounts with only a doubling of the work force.

Another interesting example of a successful new-design plant is the DEC plant in Enfield, Connecticut (see Perry, 1984). The following is the plant manager's partial list of successes, after one year of operation.

- Plant start-up on schedule
- 40 percent time reduction in the standard module process
- One-day cycle time, balanced line, continuous flow, daily shipments

- "Just-in-time" inventory system, no incoming inspection, stockrooms, or buffers in work-in-progress
- 15 inventory turns
- 6 fixed-asset turns
- 70 percent fresh lot yields for very complex modules
- 38 percent standard cost reduction for the 1985 fiscal year
- Equivalent output with half the people and half the space
- 3 percent scrap
- $500K savings on the fit-up of plant
- 40 percent reduction in overhead, resulting in break-even at 60 percent capacity

There is a good deal of additional evidence that most, if not all new-design plants are highly successful in terms of productivity, costs, and the quality of work life. Although it is not conclusive proof of success, Procter & Gamble has closed its new-design plants to researchers and others because it believes that it now enjoys a competitive advantage and it does not want to share it. Years ago, it mandated that all new plants had to be managed according to the new-design model. This has resulted in the building of over twenty new-design plants, or technician plants, as Procter & Gamble calls them. Recently Procter & Gamble went a step further and ordered all traditional plants to change to the new-design approach.

It is significant that most corporations that have tried one new-design plant have gone on to try others. It would seem that they must be meeting with favorable results. Last, it is interesting that the demand from other companies to visit new-design plants is great. Some of those that allow visitors even charge for tours and still report waiting lists. Apparently the word has gotten around that these plants have obtained impressive results, and people want to see for themselves.

A summary of positive results likely to be obtained from new-design plants is listed below. Admittedly much of these data are speculative since there is a lack of intensive studies of new plants. Still, I have collected data from over ten new plants and have had individuals and organizations report to me on results for over ten additional new plants. Thus, I feel reasonably confident that the favorable statements in this list are likely to be validated when more research is done.

- Likely improvements in work methods and procedures as a result of teams' problem solving.
- Excellent results in attracting and retaining employees because of involvement and pay.
- Cross-training leads to high levels of staffing flexibility and significant savings.
- Quality is very high due to employee motivation to do high-quality work.
- Rate of output is good due to design and motivation.
- Less staff support is needed because teams have necessary skills.
- Less supervision is needed because teams are partially self-managing.
- Low level of grievances because teams resolve issues.
- Good decision making because of teams and widespread input.
- There is a high level of skill development.

The picture presented in the above list is more positive than that presented by any other approach to participative management yet reviewed. There are two important reasons for this. First, these plants are started as new situations and so all the issues and difficulties associated with change are eliminated. Change is often the most difficult issue in putting participative management in practice. Secondly, the model is relatively congruent and it puts multiple parts of the organization into a participative mode. Thus, the problems of conflicting systems and single-system change are not present.

Problems in New-Design Plants

New-design plants are not without their conflicts and problems, although there is evidence that they perform better than traditional plants. Perkins, Nieva, and Lawler (1963), for example, report a case where significant problems developed. It is important to review the problems because they point to the limitations of participative organizations and, of course, they need to be eliminated if at all possible. In the next chapter, when consideration is given to a complete participative system, design features will be included that are targeted at eliminating some of the characteristic problems of new-design plants.

Unrealistic Expectations. The innovative employee-selection process used in many of the new-design plants has often combined with the managers' enthusiasm to create very high expectations on the part of the work force. Because of the emphasis that the selection interviews place on challenging work and autonomy, employees conclude that things will be totally different from a traditional plant. They expect their work to be interesting all the time, and they expect to be in total control of their work lives. When these expectations are not met, problems are created. Typically, workers either quit or stay and complain about the inconsistency between how they were told the work would be and how it is.

The irony is that in virtually every situation where this is a problem, the work situations have, in fact, offered more autonomy and more interesting work than is usual. Unfortunately, this is offset by the failure to fulfill the employees' expectations.

Individual Differences. People differ in their needs, skills, abilities, values, and preferences. A great deal of research has shown that not everyone responds positively to the kinds of innovations that are part of new-design plants. Some simply prefer the more traditional ways of doing things. Some, for example, do not like the group meetings that are part of the management systems. As a worker told me, "I don't care what those turkeys think, I just want to be left alone to do my job." The turkeys he was referring to were his fellow workers. This is a man who has a low need for social relationships!

In new-design plants, an effort is made to screen out those who do not fit, but some always manage to slip through. There are applicants who are not even aware of their strong orientation toward more traditional approaches, and the group interview method can fail to identify this perference. The failure of the group approach is not surprising; group interviews are not known for their validity. The result of this mismatch, in most plants, is a limited amount of turnover, particularly at start-up, and the need to work with some individuals in a more traditional manner.

In some ways, finding workers who fit the management style of the organization is probably a less severe problem in new-design plants than it is in traditional ones. A large number of workers seem to want to work in this kind of situation compared with other available opportunities. The new-design plants that have advertised for employees who want to work in a participative environment have found themselves swamped with applicants.

Role of First-Level Supervision. Probably the most frequent and most serious problem in new-design plants involves the role of the first-level supervisor (Walton and Schlesinger, 1979). In some cases, relatively traditional foremen are used; in others, no first-level supervisor is present—the assumption being that teams will be self-managing or that they will elect a leader or straw boss. In still other situations, individuals have been put in an acting-first-level supervisory position and told to work themselves out of a job within a year or so from start-up.

In almost all instances, first-level supervisors and elected leaders have complained about a lack of role clarity and confusion about what decisions they can and cannot make. Typically, they are uncomfortable with ordering and directing people, because they feel things should get done on a participative basis. But in many cases, they do not know how to function as a participative manager. Often they lack the necessary skills to help a group become a functioning team, to make decisions, and to work through issues. They also have a great deal of difficulty in deciding which decisions should be made on a participative basis and which should not.

Team leaders have ended up asking for participation on issues when they already had all the information and technical expertise that was needed to make the decision. This approach is inefficient and time-consuming, as well as pseudoparticipatory. When I have asked supervisors to justify it, they point out that they are just being participative and that they do not want to impose their answer on the group even though their answer is the correct one. Conversely, and perhaps more frequently, because many supervisors come from a traditional background, they make decisions unilaterally when they should involve the work team.

The problem is that there is no clear-cut description of the correct behavior for a first-level supervisor in a new-design plant. There are few role models for new managers to observe. Training programs are just being developed and selection methods do not exist. Therefore, the failure rate for those chosen is often high. Several organizations are trying to solve this problem by developing appropriate training programs, but to the best of my knowledge, no exemplary program exists.

Permissiveness Versus Participation. One of the hardest issues that managers in new-design plants confront is differentiating between permissiveness and participation. In most new-design plants, workers raise issues that seem to the managers to go "too far." For example, in one case, employees wanted to install a color television set in a work area. The managers considered this undesirable but had a great deal of difficulty dealing with the issue. They felt that if they said no they would be violating the participative spirit of the plant. They finally did refuse, because they felt that it would harm productivity and that it represented an example of permissive rather than participative management.

The difficulty this group of managers had is typical of problems experienced in other plants when workers have requested unusual personnel rules and work procedures. Unfortunately, the difference between what constitutes a reasonable request for the abandonment of a rule or policy and what constitutes an unreasonable request is often unclear. There is probably no way to deal with this issue in advance, but it is clear that when such issues arise, how they are dealt with can greatly influence the future of the plant. Arbitrary denials of such requests can destroy the participative spirit of the plant, just as quick acceptance of every suggestion for eliminating rules, regulations, and discipline can.

Office Personnel. Most new-design plants have had a great

deal of difficulty coming up with fresh, innovative ways to treat their office and clerical employees. They often do exactly the same jobs they would do in a more traditional plant. As a result, these employees often feel relatively unappreciated and deprived when they look at what is happening in the production areas. Although they may be supervised in a more participative manner, their life simply is not that different, even though they are told they are in a new-design organization. What is needed, of course, are innovative approaches to organizing, training, and paying people in office situations.

Some attempts have been made to improve matters, for example, by rotating employees between shipping and office jobs. The best example I know of is in a TRW plant. There, all the office clerical staff are cross-trained so that they can move from accounting to personnel and so forth. In addition, they have worked in production jobs and can help out in the factory if needed. There is one problem, however—a lack of typing skills! Interestingly, even in this innovative environment, the management employees are not cross-trained in the same way as are the clerical employees.

Personnel Function. The personnel function is usually much more important in new-design plants than in traditional ones. It tends to become a real stress point and requires a very different set of skills from those possessed by the traditional personnel manager. Since many of the typical personnel tasks are assigned to the work teams (for example, selection and pay administration), they are subtracted from the duties of the personnel department, which cannot, however, simply ignore these areas. Instead, the personnel department must work with the line organization to facilitate the accomplishment of these tasks. This requires good interpersonal skills and the ability to function as a key resource on how the new practices should be implemented.

The personnel department also needs to be experienced in job design, pay systems, training, and so on, so that other employees will have someone to consult when they need advice on implementing the philosophical concepts of the new-design plant. In many cases, personnel management ends up as a difficult, challenging job that is close to being impossible to perform. The skill demands are much greater than those required in a typical plant. Problems must be solved that have never been tackled before and that have no established solutions.

Establishing Standards. Adequate standards, in such areas as production and performance, are difficult to establish in any organization but they are particularly difficult in new organizations because they lack a track record. Thus it is not surprising that new-design plants seem to have trouble developing criteria on which to base such things as pay raises. The normal problems that are part of any start-up operation are compounded, partly because employees are typically asked to set the standards for their peers. Unless these employees receive a great deal of help, they find it hard to develop objective, challenging yardsticks for their co-workers, particularly when such matters as compensation are involved. This is hardly surprising, since they usually have little prior experience, and it is easier to be a good guy and set relatively low standards.

Plants have successfully dealt with this problem by having employees develop written tests of job knowledge and set minimum time periods that must lapse before raise applications will be considered. However, they have also failed to deal with this issue. For example, in several plants, "skill-based" pay systems have become seniority systems because of the failure to develop good standards. As an employee in one of these plants said, "We give people raises every year because they are more skilled —after all they have another year's work experience." Further investigation revealed that they typically had another year's experience doing the same work and that what they ended up with, in many cases, was one year's experience many times over.

Regression Under Pressure. At some point in the history of most plant start-ups, whether new-design or not, intense pressure for production develops. The pressure stems from the need to get the plant on-line in accordance with a predetermined, often unrealistic, production schedule. This period has proven to be particularly crucial in the life of most new-design plants (Perkins, Nieva, and Lawler, 1983). Managers tend to revert back to traditional management practices in times of crisis. They jump in and try to take charge.

Needless to say, such an act can be very damaging to the successful start-up of the new-design plant. It communicates to everyone that the new principles of management apply only when things are going well. Not all new-design plants get through this period with their commitment to participative management intact. In one instance, start-up problems, many of which were not related to management approach (for example, construction errors, such as building the ventilation system backwards in a sterile drug plant), led the plant manager to declare that the participative-management program was officially abandoned. Many problems stemmed from the fact that no preparation had been made to deal with the necessity for making some decisions, particularly technical ones, in a nonparticipative way.

Timing of Start-up Decisions. At present, no definitive timetable exists for when various activities should begin in the start-up of a new-design plant. Thus every organization that has launched such a plant has wrestled with issues such as: When should the pay system be developed? When are personnel policies to be set? When should the first employees be hired? When should work groups be established?

These are all crucial questions. Factors such as the type of technology and the skills of the employees need to be taken into account in drawing up an implementation schedule. It appears that the newer and more complex the technology is, the more slowly new management practices should be put into effect. If everything is put into effect at once, there is simply too much to learn. Indeed some plants have faltered because managers could not handle the load of learning the technology and the new management behaviors at the same time. Mastering the technology takes time and energy; so does learning new ways to manage. Where the technology is changing or complex, it may be best to think in terms of an intermediate organization design, something to be abandoned once the technology has stabilized.

Finally some plants have gotten into trouble because they tried to proceed too quickly to the final organizational design, despite the fact that it was not appropriate for the start-up period. For example, autonomous work groups have been set up as soon as production began, even though the nature of the technology did not permit stable group membership at that time.

Interface with the Rest of the Organization. In one sense, new-design plants are foreign bodies inside larger organizations. They differ in a number of important ways from the organizations that create them and to which they are responsible. For every new plant, successful or not, this has created a number of interface problems. A great deal of public attention was devoted to the General Foods' Topeka plant, but its problems are by no means unique.

At Topeka, plant-level managers came into conflict with corporate-level line and staff managers. The interface disputes at Topeka were partly caused by the threat new-design plants pose to traditional organizations. They are living demonstrations of a different way to operate, and as such they automatically raise the question of whether the rest of the organization needs to change.

Various vested interests often feel challenged by this question. Corporate staff managers, for example, may feel threatened because many issues for which they have stock answers are dealt with in an individualized manner at the plant level. Such an approach can jeopardize their job security by fostering demands for change from other parts of the organization.

Line managers in other plants may feel threatened because new-design plants operate without managers in the same or similar positions. In addition, managers in other plants may be concerned that they will have to change their whole approach to management if the new plant succeeds. Lastly, managers elsewhere in the organization may feel that their upward mobility will be hindered if the managers in the new-design plants do well and their operations are highly profitable. In fact, this is a strong possibility if the new-design managers become known as bright managers who have mastered better methods.

At this time, no organization has solved the interface issues but some are trying intriguing approaches; the most successful seem to revolve around an emphasis on decentralization and communication. On the one hand, companies using this approach stress that it is okay to be different. On the other hand, they are dealing with the communication issue in a number of ways, including seminars, task forces to study and design new plants, and frequent visits by managers from other locations to the new-design plants. This attempt cuts down on the rumors that seem to abound when new things are tried in large corporations. The case of new-design plants is no exception. I have heard some great stories about what supposedly goes on in these plants. For example, rumors have reported that there are no managers, that employees can decide to pay each other whatever they want, and that there are no work hours—people just come and go as they want.

Midlife Crisis. Most new-design plants seem to go through a "midlife crisis" somewhere between five and ten years after they are started. It usually occurs when most employees have learned all the skills, productivity growth has leveled off, the technology has been mastered and operating improvements have become hard to come by—in short, when running the plant becomes routine. At this point, many employees start asking what is next. They typically are not as enthusiastic as they used to be. They realize that they are very well off and that the plant is quite successful, but they would like more growth, responsibility, and excitement.

At this point, they start looking for a "second generation model." Most of the plants have not found this new model and have stuck with the original one as have the Procter & Gamble plants. They have continued to be effective (for over fifteen years, in the case of the older ones) but there is often the feeling that more could be accomplished. A few have successfully moved toward a high-involvement management approach in order to fully tap the resources of their people.

The list below summarizes problems that are likely to occur as a result of the new-design model. Overall, many of the problems are the type that success brings—in other words—the right kind of problems.

- Average pay per employee is higher but leaner staffing may reduce total salary costs.

- Training costs are high because of cross-training and team training.
- The need for support personnel is high in personnel area, but not in others.
- Expectations for organizational change can be too high because of the selection process and philosophy.
- Resistance by middle management can occur even though there are few of them.
- Resistance by staff support groups can occur even though there are few of them.
- Expectations for personal growth and development can be too high given the limited time to cross-train.
- Relation to other parts of the organization can be a problem.
- Time is lost in team meeting, and decision process can be slow.

It is too early to make a final assessment of the new-design model. Nevertheless, there seems little question that it will continue to spread to other organizations and within organizations as they start new plants. It is now well-known that these plants are quite successful and the know-how for starting them is widely spread throughout many organizations. In short, the approach or model is no longer a curiosity—it is a piece of established management technology that a number of companies have mastered. The challenge at the moment is to improve on the model so that the problems are reduced. It provides a good starting point for our discussion of what a completely participative organization should look like. As we shall see, many of its dysfunctions can be eliminated by incorporating additional features that do more to move power, knowledge, information, and rewards to lower levels.

11

How High-Involvement Management Works

Now that we have reviewed the major participative-management approaches, we are in a position to discuss how all the pieces fit together. We can describe what a participatively managed organization must look like if it is to operate in a way that jointly maximizes the involvement of all employees and organizational effectiveness. We have identified most of the puzzle pieces; the challenge now is to put them together to form a high-involvement organization.

One of the most important points stressed throughout the book concerns the need for congruence among the different parts of an organization. Even though the participative approaches considered so far do not affect rewards, information, knowledge, and power in a complete and congruent way, each one produces some positive results. Therefore, we have to be optimistic about what is possible if we develop organizations that are participative in every way. By this I mean organizations that give rewards, information, knowledge, and power to all employees so that everyone can be involved in the organization's performance.

There are no perfect examples of high-involvement organizations. The new plants discussed in the previous chapter are the best models available. They are designed and managed in a way that is generally congruent with high-involvement management. Thus, they can serve as a good basis for outlining what high-involvement management should look like. Another good example is provided by People Express Airline; it too has built into its systems a participative approach to management. In the following discussion we will review the critical organizational features and show how they should be designed in order to be congruent with high levels of employee involvement.

Management Philosophy and Core Values

High-involvement management starts with beliefs about people that support their being involved. Douglas McGregor (1960) was the first to articulate the importance of the assumptions we make about people. They turn out to be the basis for the design of many organizational features. Many recent publications on effective organizations also have stressed that organizations need to have clearly articulated guiding principles, philosophies, and core values (Peters and Waterman, 1982; O'Toole, 1985). Effective organizations have particularly well-articulated statements that are congruent with the way the organization is run.

A high-involvement organization's core values and principles must be congruent with the idea of employee involvement and responsibility for decision making. Examples of assumptions that are often the basis for participative approaches to organizing and managing people are listed below.

Human Relations
- People should be treated fairly and with respect.
- People want to participate.
- When people participate, they accept change.
- When people participate, they are more satisfied and committed to the organization.

Human Resources
- People are a valuable resource because they have ideas and knowledge.

- When people have input in decisions, better solutions are developed.
- Organizations should make a long-term commitment to the development of people because it makes them more valuable to the organization.

High Involvement

- People can be trusted to make important decisions about their work activities.
- People can develop the knowledge to make important decisions about the management of their work activities.
- When people make decisions about the management of their work, the result is greater organizational effectiveness.

The human relations approach is typical of those used by major U.S. organizations. It encourages certain kinds of participative activities. Organizations that make these assumptions are likely to have attitude-survey programs, quality-circle programs, and other suggestion programs.

The human resource approach takes participation one step further and argues for moving more information, power, and knowledge downward in the organization. It stops short, however, of delegating important decisions to lower-level employees. Thus, it is suggestive of approaches like gainsharing and certain kinds of job redesign.

The high-involvement approach accepts both the human relations and human resource assumptions and takes them further. It is consistent with the type of practices used in new-design plants and will be used here as the basis for developing a high-involvement management model.

In most organizations, it is important that members of the organization articulate their own assumptions. The ones presented here are not meant to be adopted by organizations. Rather, they are illustrative of the kind of assumptions that can be made in organizations. The key to a successful high-involvement organization is that the assumptions be developed by members of that organization, that they be widely known, and that they be used as a touchstone for decisions about adopting particular practices. Examples of statements that are taken from the philosophies of companies are listed below. Statements like these need to guide the development of the other parts of high-involvement organizations.

Forest Products Company

- Work should be satisfying and employees should feel they are making a contribution.
- We expect participative goal setting at all levels.
- By involving people we can achieve excellence.

Rolm

- To create a great place to work.

Signetics

- Managers (should) allow people to do their jobs unhindered.

GTE

- We will strive to make employee involvement an integral part of our management process.

Organizational Structure

High-involvement management requires an organizational structure that is very similar to that found in new-design plants, with few levels of management and light staffing, especially in the area of staff support. Many of the staff support activities should be accomplished by the production people. The remaining staff groups should be largely in a consulting and training role. An important objective for them is the transfer of their expertise to other employees.

The reason for having a flat structure should be obvious. The best way to assure that decisions are made at lower levels is to have very few levels of management, so that managers cannot make all the decisions. The struggle that occurs in traditional organizations—to hoard decisions because there are so few per person—is best eliminated by eliminating levels of management. Earlier, it was mentioned that AT&T had to face this when it started job enrichment. Other telephone companies are finding that eliminating one level of management is not enough; three or four levels need to go. High-involvement plants may need only two levels of management—the plant manager and the team leader.

I remember very vividly a plant manager who said that he firmly believed in pushing decisions down. I asked him if he was planning to start a job-enrichment activity in his plant. His response was that before he could do that he needed some decisions pushed down to his level, which was five levels above the production workers. In his case, as in many other extensive hierarchies, it is almost impossible to push decisions down. If they were pushed down, then what would the higher levels do? After all, there are only so many decisions to be made.

The fundamental grouping approach in a high-involvement organization should be toward organizational units that feel responsible for a particular product or customer. The alternative of structuring around function (such as engineering or accounting) is incongruent with high-involvement management because it creates a situation where individuals are performing their own particular specialty; they have no identification with the product or contact with the customer. This creates the need for hierarchy and extensive control systems to assure that the different functions work together to deliver the product or service that the customer wants. It also limits the degree to which they understand the business and are motivated to produce a high-quality product or service.

In large corporations, high-involvement management almost inevitably means a decentralized organization that is structured around businesses. It does not mean large, highly specialized corporate staffs and organizing around such functions as manufacturing, finance, sales, and marketing. The old AT&T is a classic example of an organization designed around functional areas; the different parts only came together at the top. TRW, 3M, and Honeywell, to mention a few, are examples of companies that are organized around businesses and, as a result, are better positioned for high-involvement management.

In high-involvement organizations, many mini-enterprises need to be created so that employees are part of a business they can relate to. These mini-enterprises should sell products and services either to each other, if this is appropriate, or to outside customers. This is the best way to break down large plants into areas small enough for people to identify with, and where they have a line of sight to overall performance. It is crucial to create a situation where people face a customer who can give them feedback and react to their particular product or service, whether this customer is a member of the same organization or not. Each part of the organization should have customer responsibility of some type. Only then can people get a sense of motivation and satisfaction from serving a customer.

The most effective installation I have seen of the mini-enterprise concept is in the Cummins Engine facility, mentioned earlier. The plant is broken up into seven businesses, each of which makes its own products and has its own financial performance results. Talking with the employees is very impressive. They can tell you cost and other information that is normally the concern of management. In short, they care about *their* business and this pays off for Cummins.

Xerox has done an excellent job of combining the mini-enterprise approach with a practice called "competitive bench marking." They study competing businesses so that they have a clear idea of what they must do to be effective. They also monitor the performance of competitors so that Xerox employees can get good feedback about their relative performance.

It is particularly important in larger high-involvement organizations to have a representative council or committee to deal with important organization-wide matters. These councils are often present in new-design plants. They can be elected or appointed by management, but they must represent people from different levels and different parts of the organization.

These groups deal with varying issues, including hours of work, personnel policies, scheduling production work, communication, and planning major introductions of new products and new equipment. General Motors has committed to involving groups like these in important policy decisions in its new Saturn project. Joint union-management task forces have already played a role in the design of the Saturn organization. They deal with anything that has an organization-wide impact. The purpose of these groups is to allow organizational decisions to be influenced by representatives from different parts of the organization and to facilitate acceptance and communication concerning the issues. An alternative is to appoint a task force to work on each specific issue. This approach has been used very successfully by parts of Honeywell in its participative-management activities.

Job Design

The type of job design follows directly from the organizational structure and the technology. It should involve individually enriched jobs or teams. As was discussed earlier, the choice between individual enrichment and teams should be based on technology and the degree to which an individual can be given responsibility for a whole task or a whole piece of work. If an individual can be given a whole task, then individual enrichment is usually the best choice because it avoids the complexities and training that are involved in developing effective teams. Often, however, there is no choice: teams are needed because an individual cannot personally produce a product or service and relate to a customer. For example, individuals simply cannot run a chemical plant or even a paper machine and, as a result, a team is needed.

One other consideration is relevant—the psychological needs of the employees. If teams are used, it is important to staff the organization with people who like social contact, so that the interaction involved in team work will be pleasurable to them and not a source of discontent.

Problem-Solving Groups

Task forces are needed, at times, to deal with key issues. Production, service, or quality problems that involve several areas are good candidates for task force solutions. These task forces should get the problem-solving and group-process training that are common in quality circles, but there is no need for an elaborate quality-circle structure in most high-involvement organizations. The normal functions of quality circles can be done by the teams or by the participative-council structure. What remains are certain special issues that need to be addressed by a cross-section of people from the plant. This can best be done by temporary task forces that make recommendations to the existing structure. Consistent with this view is my observation that no new-design plants have found the need for quality circles.

Information System

The information system is the key to effective coordination and feedback in any organization but is particularly crucial in a high-involvement system. Since many of the levels of hierarchy and staff support are gone, the information system must provide the capability for people to coordinate and manage themselves. Even with the best of intentions, in the absence of an effective information system, employees cannot become self-regulating. For example, a key to the success of the Cummins Engine plant, mentioned earlier, is the cost-information system that tells each mini-enterprise how it is performing.

The availability of inexpensive computing and the capability to create networks among computers makes it much easier to structure a high-involvement organization these days. Computers provide the potential of putting large amounts of information in the hands of individuals or groups throughout the organization. They can directly communicate with each other in order to coordinate their activities. It is now possible for people to work on problems that in the past required a central staff group or an outside group because the data were not generally available in the organization (Naisbitt and Aburdene, 1985).

Although some have suggested that the information revolution will lead organizations toward greater centralization, new research by my colleague, Allan Mohrman, suggests just the opposite. Because of the capability it provides, information about the business can and almost always does spread to new parts of the organization and this can allow people to do new kinds of work and to be involved in new decisions.

The information system needs to be open to all members

of the organization, so that they can get the kind of financial, production, and other information that they need. Mini-enterprises or teams need to get information about how effectively they are performing and how their performance compares to standards and to their competitors. It also needs to tell them how they are servicing their customers. Feedback from customers is particularly crucial. In the DEC Enfield, Connecticut, plant, a toll-free telephone number on the shop floors allows customers to call the team that built their product. This approach serves two ends. It provides feedback and it shows the employees how serious top management is about doing high-quality work.

The goals and standards of most information systems should be participatively set and based on input from each work area. This will promote individual commitment to high performance and the perception of feedback as relevant and motivating.

The information system should not only include data about financial operating results; it should also include information on the human system. In particular, survey data should be regularly collected and fed back to individuals in the organizations. The survey-feedback model is particularly appropriate for handling this information. The widespread use of computer terminals could significantly improve the feedback process. Individuals throughout the organization could respond to survey questions on terminals and almost immediate feedback could be given regarding how particular work groups and individuals compare to the rest of the organization. So far, no organization I know of does this, but it offers the potential for real-time problem solving and gives the organization a much better opportunity to sense how people feel about certain critical decisions.

The information system should be decentralized. That is, it should provide the information that individuals and work areas need to coordinate, manage, and evaluate their own performance. It also should provide an individual with a good sense of how well the whole organization is performing. Great care should be taken to ensure that each individual understands the overall operation of the organization and has the kind of financial, planning, and market information that will allow him or her to understand how the business is doing. This information is crucial in helping the individual to identify with and care about the organization.

From a hardware point of view, the high-involvement approach requires broadly distributing computing capability throughout the organization. This creates the possibility of all individuals having access to information about the organization's performance. With the rapid adoption of computers throughout organizations, the potential for sharing information and empowering individuals who typically have not had decision-making responsibility is enormous. Secretaries, production employees, and many others who previously did not have the information to influence certain decisions can now have an influence because of computers. In many respects, the computer revolution enables organizations to be structured around high-involvement principles.

Physical and Technical Design

High-involvement organizations need a particular physical layout. First, they need to be egalitarian and to meet people's needs for a safe, pleasant work environment. Perhaps the most controversial point here is the issue of egalitarian surroundings. This is done to reinforce the classless structure of the organization and to impress upon people that decisions are based on expertise, not hierarchy. Thus, such status symbols as reserved parking spaces, separate entrances, executive dining rooms, and special offices are not acceptable. Many California high-tech firms such as Apple, Intel, Rolm, and Advanced Micro Devices (AMD) carry the egalitarian workplace one step further. They encourage employees to socialize together by staging elaborate parties and having recreational facilities such as volleyball courts and even hot tubs!

The normal dress code, in which people at different levels of power wear different clothes, is also not appropriate in high-involvement organizations. For example, in Honda's United States plants, everyone wears a Honda uniform. In other plants, no one wears ties or uses other symbols of power, such as silver water bottles, carpets, large desks, and receptionists.

Overall, the physical layout should reflect the organizational structure and the job design. If teams are involved, just as in new-design plants, the physical layout should naturally create team boundaries and areas of team ownership. Mini-enterprises should also be physically separated to provide them with a sense of identity.

Some new plants are particularly good examples of how to design a physical setting to fit high-involvement management. For example, Digital Equipment plants have no reserved parking spaces or other perquisites. If top management wants to park next to the front door they can arrive early enough to get a space! The effect is to create a psychologically more egalitarian culture. This same approach has been taken in the new U.S. plants built by Honda and Nissan. It is a notable contrast to most traditional U.S. auto plants, where managers have special parking garages where their cars are cleaned and serviced. Not only does this reinforce management power, it deprives the executives of the chance to examine what it is really like to own one of their cars (for example, cold starts and servicing).

There are also some interesting examples of office buildings that are designed for participation. In some financial-service organizations (notably banks and insurance companies), the same principle has been used to create service units that have their own "turf." Finally, there is the example of Union Carbide's new corporate headquarters, which minimizes status differences between management levels by providing similar offices and furniture. Union Carbide claims a significant out-of-pocket savings from egalitarianism because it does not have to change offices and perquisites around every time someone changes jobs.

In general, high-involvement organizations should have small locations. A basic principle of involvement is to create small units that can be self-managing and that people can identify with. The large multi-thousand-person plant or office structure is the exact opposite of the kind of physical structure that supports a high-involvement work model. Sometimes these are necessary because of the advantages that they offer. If this is the case, then they should be broken down into mini-enterprises and everything possible should be done to avoid the depersonalization, communication problems, and powerlessness that people feel when working in such large structures.

Reward System

A high-involvement organization needs a different reward system than traditional organizations. Specifically, it calls for skill-based pay, gainsharing, profit sharing, employee ownership, flexible benefits, an all-salary work force, and open, participative decision processes.

Skill-based pay is a critical element in developing knowledge and in communicating one of the high-involvement core values: personal growth. It has been shown to be effective in new plants (Lawler and Ledford, 1985). In high-involvement organizations, it needs to be expanded to pay for economic-knowledge skills as well as normal production skills. It also needs to include managers. In most new plants it has not covered managers, although I am now working with several plants that are extending it to managers. In a fully developed skill-based pay system, it should be quite possible for a highly skilled production team member to make more than a manager (particularly a new one) simply because the team member knows more.

The reward system also needs to include some form or forms of gainsharing. Our discussion of gainsharing pointed out its many advantages. It offers a vehicle for pushing rewards throughout the organization. This can increase the motivation level and help everyone relate to the larger unit of which they are part. It provides people with ongoing excitement about the business that is absent when their economic fate is not tied to the success of their organization.

One manager of a new plant told me recently that as a new plant matures, much of the work becomes rather routine but there can always be the excitement of how "we are doing" as a business. This excitement can be made real to people when their economic situation reflects and is tied into how well the business is doing.

In large organizations, a profit-sharing plan may need to

be combined with gainsharing. Profit sharing can provide a backup to local-unit gainsharing plans. It is unreasonable to expect much motivation to result from profit sharing in a large organization because the performance-reward connection is usually too weak. However, it can give an organization a sense of unity and it can communicate to everyone that they are part of the business. It can also help avoid the negative situation that comes up in many corporations: high profits for the corporation, large bonuses for the executives, but nothing for most members of the organization.

By combining gainsharing and profit sharing, organizations can also vary their labor cost in relation to their ability to pay. In too many U.S. organizations, the only way to reduce labor costs is to lay people off; this makes it difficult to talk about employment security and it insulates people from the realities of business except in the case of an extreme downturn.

Stock ownership is desirable as a further approach to tying employees' rewards to the success of the company. In large companies, this may only be a symbolic act because of the indirect connection between individual performance and the value of the stock. Nevertheless, it can be an important symbolic act because it communicates to everyone that they are not just employees in the organization—they are, in fact, owners. Some organizations even require all employees to buy at least one hundred shares of stock before they become employees. This has worked well, so far, for People Express employees (they have made money) and the company (they have raised capital). Other companies handle this issue through stock-purchase plans and other vehicles that encourage individuals to buy stock in the organization. Complete employee ownership of the organization is also possible. It has worked well in a number of cases (such as Weirton Steel), but it is not a stand-alone prescription for organizational effectiveness, as some have assumed it might be. It needs to be combined with other participative-management practices.

The reward system should also allow individuals to choose their fringe benefits (Lawler, 1981). With flexible benefit plans, individuals choose a package of fringe benefits, cash, and other rewards. This particular approach reinforces the fact that people differ in their needs and that the organization considers them to be mature and capable of making important decisions. TRW, American Can, and a number of other organizations have already installed flexible-benefit plans and the results have been very positive. It tends to reduce turnover and to build individual commitment to the organization. It also fits nicely with an egalitarian pay structure in which all employees are on salary and have the same benefit options open to them.

In traditional organizations, pay decisions are made in a top-down manner and are, in general, kept secret. This is incongruent with a participative approach, which calls for open information and widespread input into decisions. Although this may sound impractical, I have seen it work effectively at both the management and employee level. For example, in many new plants, work teams openly discuss each other's pay and make decisions about it. In one company I worked with, the same thing occurred among the top-level managers. The result in the new plants and with the executives was the same: a good discussion took place and responsible, effective decisions were made, which were highly creditable.

Personnel Policies

Many of the personnel policies in high-involvement organizations need to be developed to fit the local work force. This can be a particularly important activity for the organization-wide task forces and the participative councils mentioned earlier. They can deal with such issues as hours of work, flex-time, types of benefits offered, layoffs, discipline, and other issues that are typically decided by management. It is particularly important that these issues be dealt with on a participative basis so that individuals will be committed to the policies.

Where possible, these policies should allow individuals a choice and recognize the differences among people. Thus, such practices as flex-time and even giving groups the ability to decide who works on a particular shift and what kinds of benefits will be offered, make a great deal of sense. The TRW plant in

Lawrence, Kansas, provides a good example of employees deciding who will work on the different shifts: teams of employees are asked to staff all three shifts on whatever basis they decide. They are, of course, required to meet production demands.

Stability of employment is a key issue in any participatively managed organization (Rosow, 1984). Without some guarantee concerning stability of employment, it is difficult for individuals to make the kind of commitment that will lead to an effective high-involvement organization. When individuals fear layoffs, for example, they are hesitant to make suggestions that will reduce labor cost and to develop unique skills and capabilities that can be utilized only by their organization. They are also more likely to leave if they see a better offer somewhere else. Of course, in some cyclical business situations, stability of employment simply cannot be guaranteed and all the organization can say is that it gives stability a high priority.

Most of the organizations that practice participative management are hesitant to lay off employees for a somewhat selfish reason. They have invested large amounts of money in training and developing them, and they are hesitant to liquidate this investment, so they do a number of things to assure that they do not lose their valuable employees. For example, when work surges come, they hire temporary employees so they are not overstaffed on a permanent basis. When layoffs are necessary, they do work-sharing rather than laying off people.

Where reductions or layoffs in the work force are necessary, it is possible to have the participative council or a task force decide on a layoff policy. In my experience, these groups behave very responsibly when given this responsibility. For example, they typically do not simply lay off based on seniority. A common practice is to first ask for volunteers and then to consider work-week reduction, so that the pay reduction will be broadly shared in the organization. As a final resort, they lay off people based on their performance and skills. Seniority typically becomes an issue only if people are comparable in performance.

There is a tie-in here with gainsharing and profit sharing. Most organizations that have gainsharing give highest priority to stability of employment. This means that if there is a choice between paying a bonus or laying people off, the organization will choose to pay no bonus. In this respect, the gainsharing plan becomes a potential absorber of the ups and downs of the business cycle.

Career System

The skill-based concept and the cross-training that are necessary to make a high-involvement work situation effective also make the career system a particularly important organizational feature. In order to be effective, it requires both clear communication of the options available and counseling for individuals about what skills they should learn and what their long-term careers can be. Some of this counseling can be handled within the work teams and immediate work area. It may also require some staff specialists to help with communication about job openings and to facilitate people assessing their own skills, abilities, and career interest. Overall, the career system needs to recognize that people differ in the kind of career orientation they have and it needs to help individuals find a career direction that fits their particular preferences. This, of course, must be balanced with the organization's needs for skills.

Because high-involvement organizations are flat, there is much less chance for the traditional upward career. On the other hand, career tracks that involve a great deal of learning and growth can be developed. Skill-based pay for managers as well as for production employees comes into play here. It is a way to provide financial and career growth for managers even though the organization is relatively flat. One thing that most high-involvement work structures cannot tolerate is the individual who simply wants to do the same job year after year. This person blocks the movement of others and provides a poor model.

Selection System

The selection system is a particularly critical feature of a high-involvement organization. Clearly, this type of organization is not for all individuals: it takes a particular orientation toward career and toward work, and, most importantly, toward learning, growing, and developing as a human being. This is inherent in the very structure of a high-involvement work organization and must be present in all members of the organization. Closely related to this is the willingness and desire to be responsible for one's own behavior. If the organization is team-based, it also requires good interpersonal-process skills and the willingness to work well in groups.

The selection system in the organization faces a big task. It must staff the organization with individuals who have the right kind of needs and skills to operate effectively in a high-involvement setting. Unfortunately, there are no magic devices, although there are several key features that can help the selection process to go well.

First, job applicants should be given a very extensive, realistic job preview, as is typically done in new-design plants. This allows individuals to decide whether they can work effectively in this kind of work setting. It is also advisable to have the people from the potential work area involved in the selection decision. These people can provide valuable input as to whether the person will fit. Further, when they recommend someone to be employed they become committed to seeing that the person is successful. Thus, their involvement has the double advantage of committing them to seeing that the person works out and utilizing their judgment as to the person's possible success.

A work team interview is a good way to give the applicant a clear sense of the way a high-involvement organization is run. Not surprisingly, some applicants are not comfortable with the process and decide to withdraw their application. This process not only gives the team members input to decisions but also allows them to see the applicant function in a group situation. Those organizations that use this approach do not rely on it as the only selection approach. Other tests are needed to determine skills and, of course, background checks are needed. Finally, it is important to note that most work teams need to be trained in how to do this type of interviewing and safeguards against discrimination need to be in place.

Training Orientation

A major feature of a high-involvement organization must be a high level of training capability and commitment. Its very essence is learning, growth, and development. The organization therefore needs to do everything possible to facilitate individuals' adding to their skills and developing as human beings. In addition to all the necessary kinds of technical training, it is very important that interpersonal-skill and problem-solving training be provided. If problem solving is going to take place throughout the organization it usually means group meetings. In order for these to be effective, individuals throughout the organization must have the ability to problem solve and to quickly form into effective decision-making groups.

There is one other area of education that is typically not included in organizational training packages but that is critical for high-involvement organizations. Unfortunately, many employees in the United States lack a good understanding of the basic economic situation that their organization faces. In essence they are asked to compete in a very difficult game, but they do not know how the score is kept. They also lack education about how the financial-information system in their own organization works. It is critical that this be overcome with economic education. This is such an important skill that it should be included in the skill-based pay system, so that as individuals acquire more economic knowledge of the business their pay goes up. Employees need to understand the competitive situation that their organization faces and how the organization is dealing with it. Competition is a powerful motivation, but it is effective only when individuals know who they are competing against, what they have to do to win, and how they are faring compared with the competition. Just like in sports, the game is most interesting when you keep score!

The heavy emphasis on training and development ties directly into the skill-based pay system. Without this strong emphasis, skill-based pay is a sham because individuals are not in a position to acquire the rewarded skills. Similarly, without skill-based pay the training emphasis is somewhat of a sham because the reward system of the organization does not support it. Instead, the reward system is saying that the only way to move up significantly in pay is to get promoted. This message is okay for an organization that wants to put power at the top and that wants most people to strive for the few top-level positions. It has no place in a high-involvement organization with its emphasis on power moving toward expertise and on people throughout the organization continually learning, growing, and developing.

Leadership Style

Leadership in a high-involvement work organization is a different activity than it is in a traditional workplace. Both the task of the manager and the responses of the employees need to be quite different. In the traditional organization, leadership is based on the manager having the decision-making power, the information, the rewards, and in some cases, the expertise. As a result of this, the manager is able to tell people what to do and to command their fear if not their respect. What is needed is a manager or administrator—not a leader (Zalcznik, 1977).

Here I am using the term *leader* to apply to someone who inspires loyalty, commitment, and motivation through his or her personal style and behavior. Some people have referred to this as *charismatic leadership,* but that may not be the best term. Too often, the term *charismatic leadership* gets associated with leaders who develop unquestioning, totally committed relationships with their followers (for example, Hitler and various cult leaders). High-involvement management requires leaders who energize people in ways that support self-motivation (Bennis and Nanus, 1985); leaders who help people move in positive directions, where questioning and debate is acceptable and part of the organization's search for the best answer (Burns, 1978); leaders who help the organization know the right things to do rather than helping it do things right.

In high-involvement organizations, the key positions need to be staffed by leaders. Traditional managerial behaviors are not needed because of the self-regulatory nature of the design.

Leadership, however, is needed to provide a sense of purpose and direction as well as to shape the organization's culture and decision processes.

In a high-involvement organization, information is widely shared, as are expertise and rewards—thus, the important traditional power bases are not present in the managers' role. The managers have to rely on other means for influencing behavior and shaping the direction of the organization. In some instances, they can rely on their superior expertise and information to influence and direct the organization. In many cases, however, the managers may not have the greatest expertise and must direct the decision making to the individual or groups that have the information and expertise. This is one of the most important functions of the manager in a high-involvement organization, as is seeing that a healthy process that produces good decisions is used.

Studies of effective leaders suggest that perhaps the most powerful impact they can have on high-involvement organizations is through their vision of the organization (Bennis and Nanus, 1985). This vision helps the organization set goals for itself, provides a sense of what the organization can be and what people's roles in it can be. It also states philosophies and values that are accepted by members of the organization. It gives them a sense of direction and a purpose for their work lives.

The behavior that a leader uses to accomplish this, by necessity, has to vary from situation to situation. But a few things can be said about it. It seems to be very important to establish symbols and phrases that capture the nature of the organization and the way it is to be run. Don Burr, the president of People Express Airline, has made good use of symbols and language in shaping the airline's culture. In order to emphasize the airline's participative-management approach, all employees are called managers. Budgets are virtually nonexistent because they indicate that people cannot be trusted to spend what is right. They are also often padded and lead people to spend unnecessarily in order to retain their budget. In addition, as noted earlier, the planes are called soft assets while the employees are referred to as hard assets. In order to emphasize the service orientation of the airline, all passengers are called *customers,* never passengers. When Renn Zaphiropoulos became head of a major group at Xerox, he personally bought black paint and proceeded to paint over the names on all reserved parking spaces. He also identified the eagle as a symbol for his division, because it soars high. Prior to his taking over, the division had, to put it mildly, failed to take off (for other examples, see O'Toole, 1985; Peters and Austin, 1985).

Key activities and events need to be scheduled that recognize the accomplishments of the organization and bring to life its core values. In this sense, the leader is responsible for managing the organization's culture as well as for shaping its long-term goals and orientation. A good example of a dramatic event was staged by the president of a high-technology firm. Frustrated with the low goals his subordinates had set for themselves, he asked them to be in the company parking lot early the next morning. He did not tell them what to expect, but he did tell them to wear old clothes. When they arrived the next morning, they found a helicopter waiting to take them to an isolated beach on the California coast. They were told that they would spend the morning climbing a high cliff above the beach. There was some complaining, and doubts were expressed about whether they could actually do it; but by helping each other they did manage to climb the cliff. Upon reaching the top, the president talked about the importance of setting high goals and the fact that people can often accomplish more than they think they can, just as they had that morning.

Overall, managers in high-involvement organizations need a particular set of leadership skills that will allow them to do four critical things for the organization.

1. Build trust and openness.
2. Provide a vision and communicate it.
3. Move decisions to the proper location.
4. Empower others.

This list, which is partially based on the work of my colleagues, Warren Bennis and Burt Nanus (1985), captures what great leaders do in high-involvement organizations. Let us look at each of them.

Trust is desirable in all organizations, but it is essential in high-involvement organizations. Openness and sticking to a vision are the best ways to build trust. Thus, the leader who has a vision, communicates it clearly, *and* then lives up to it establishes trust. The issue here is essentially one of the leaders' acting consistently with the way they talk. There is little room for inconsistency. The leaders must not only preach; they must practice what they preach. The start-up of the new Ohio Honda plant is a good example of this. Management preached quality and the workers knew they meant it when production began. They knew it because they controlled the pace of the assembly line and were told to take *all* the time they needed to do the job right. Only a few cars came off the line at first, but they were of top quality, equal to or better than those built in Japan. This quality standard continues to the present day.

In the high-involvement organization, the leader must preach and practice openness as well as move decisions to where the relevant expertise is found. As one manager at Xerox commented to another, we must "walk like we talk." He added that it is not easy to do. For example, when an employee asks questions about business operations, the managers cannot dismiss them as "none of your business." They must be fully answered and the individual must feel rewarded for asking it. Trust in an organization starts with a trusted leader and builds from there. Without trust in management, there cannot be trust throughout the organization.

Good leadership can be felt at all levels in an organization. It gives people direction, energy, and a sense of competence—in other words, "empowerment." It is the result of leaders effectively communicating a vision, building trust, and allowing others to use their competencies. Good leaders value other people learning, growing, developing, and exercising competence-based power. When they demonstrate this, it causes people to reach for higher levels of competence and to be motivated by their growth.

Finally, it is important to mention that group-process and interpersonal-process skills are particularly important for leaders in high-involvement work organizations. Yes, walking around is important (Peters and Waterman, 1982), but it is not enough. Leaders must be able to engage people in meaningful conversation and quickly develop a sense of the way things are going. One Cummins Engine plant manager stated this very well when I asked him how he spends his time. He said he spends about 95 percent of it monitoring the communication and decision processes in his organization. What was he looking for? Breakdowns in involvement, mistreatment of employees, people feeling left out, and so on.

Much of the leadership in high-involvement organizations gets accomplished through working with people in groups and in team settings. As a result, it is particularly crucial that managers have expertise in aiding groups to make decisions and in facilitating group problem solving.

Role of Unions

There is a definite role for unions in high-involvement management. It is, however, quite different from the traditional role unions have had in the United States. Our discussion of QWL projects suggested some ways in which union and management can cooperate to increase organizational effectiveness and the quality of work life. In high-involvement management, much more change is required. In most respects, the traditional collective bargaining adversarial role needs to be completely abandoned. The union needs to become a partner with management.

Unions can bring a considerable amount to any partnership. They represent the legitimate representatives of many employees and, as such, they can speak for employees in a number of settings. As has already been established in the case of Chrysler, their officers can sit on boards of directors. Unions can also play a major role in keeping management "honest" with respect to participative management. They can be sure that there is no backsliding and that all the relevant voices are heard on critical issues. Finally, they can support decisions in a way that adds credibility and aids acceptance.

In this new role, it is possible to imagine a one-page contract that serves as a general framework and guideline. Traditional contractual issues would be handled on an ongoing problem-solving basis, as decisions are required. There would be no such thing as contract expiration date; instead, the contract would always be open for change, as needed. Pay would be handled through gainsharing and profit sharing. In short, a much more flexible union-management relationship is envisioned in which the union aids in the movement of power, knowledge, information, and rewards to all the employees of the organization.

The General Motors' Saturn project represents a good example of how unions can facilitate high-involvement management. In this start-up, the UAW and General Motors have been partners from the beginning. A joint design committee developed a philosophy, worked on the sociotechnical layout, and aided in the site selection process. Their design calls for gainsharing, teams, skill-based pay, and even a joint union-management structure for setting policies and business strategy. This effort seems to go a long way toward involving all employees—union and nonunion—in the business.

Putting It All Together

The key to success for high-involvement organizations is the same as for any organization: consistency and congruence. Individual practices must fit together and must affect everyone in the same way. The features discussed in this chapter all contribute to building an organization in which power, information, knowledge, and rewards are moved downward. They meet the twin criteria of affecting the total organization and of being consistent in their approach to dealing with people. The reward system encourages employees to develop their skills; the information system gives them the foundation they need to use their skills; the training and selection system helps them develop their skills; and the work design gives them the power and tasks that utilize their skills.

When all these features are combined, they produce a congruent high-involvement organization that is distinctly different from existing organizations. In this sense, it may seem like an idealistic model that involves considerable risk. Quite the contrary is true. It is merely a complete development of the idea of moving power, rewards, knowledge, and information to the lowest levels of the organization. It may appear to be a high-risk approach, but in many respects it is low-risk because it is congruent and covers the entire organization. It is much riskier to move only some of these features downward, thereby creating an incongruent organization. It is even riskier to continue to practice traditional management in a changing environment.

High-involvement management is the best way to make many American organizations competitive in an international arena where some countries have a competitive advantage through raw materials, others through low labor cost, and still others through geographic position. High-involvement management is the competitive advantage available to countries with educated, achievement-oriented work forces who want to perform effectively, whose core values support participative decision making, and who can engage in substantial amounts of self-regulation. At this point, it is more of a concept than a reality, but many of the practices have been proven in the sense that they have worked in new plants and in plants with gainsharing. The key question at this point is not whether high-involvement organizations will work. It is how to create such organizations.

12

Managing the Change to a High-Involvement Organization

It is much easier to talk about what a high-involvement organization should look like than it is to describe how to create one. Over the last twenty years I have participated in more than a hundred change efforts that were directed toward increasing employee participation. One conclusion is clear: there are no cut-and-dried formulas. The best that we can come up with are some general guidelines that can help to direct a change effort. Anyone who offers a pat formula is, in my opinion, highly suspect. A look at the major change efforts underway at General Motors, Ford, Honeywell, Motorola, Xerox, and TRW, to mention a few, indicates that they all differ in important ways. They differ because although they share the same general objectives, they start from different places and the strategists working on each have different ideas about how to do it. Nevertheless, there are some common issues that every change effort must deal with.

Change Needs a Reason

The starting point for every change program needs to be the question, why change? There are many possible answers to this question but only one is given in most successful change efforts: simply stated, it is that the organization's business strategy and ultimately its survival depends on it. Other reasons—such as, it is right, just, or more fun—simply do not seem to be as effective a basis for change efforts, because they do not mobilize the effort that occurs when business success or survival is at stake.

The successful corporate-wide change efforts I have discussed so far are all based on business need. For example, General Motors and Ford have based their programs on their need to improve product quality and reduce costs in order to compete successfully with offshore auto manufacturers. Similarly, Xerox's program began because it was not competing effectively in the copier market: in order to do so, it needed to reduce cost and improve quality. Finally, Motorola realized it needed to move toward high-technology products (leaving behind its problem-ridden consumer television business). This meant it also needed to move toward a participative-management approach that includes gainsharing and work teams.

Although a reason for change is needed, an organization does not have to be desperate in order to undertake a successful major change effort. If the organization's condition is too bad, it may be unable to change because it does not have sufficient time and resources. Honeywell, Cummins Engine, and Mead are good examples of change efforts that began long before their business situation represented a serious problem.

It is hardly surprising that change efforts require a compelling reason if they are to be successful. Change involves hard work, is disruptive, and can have a negative effect on a number of people. In the case of a participative-management change, old behaviors have to be abandoned, people often have to be replaced because they cannot adapt, and a large financial investment is required.

There Are Many Roads to Participative Systems

The literature is full of suggestions about how to start change efforts designed to move from traditional systems to participative ones. Philosophy development, survey feedback, job-enrichment programs, quality circles, self-managing teams, and team building are among the most frequently suggested approaches. If the views suggested so far are correct, any one of these can be a place to start. The key is to begin with an issue that is of concern to people, and where change can be introduced. This point stems directly from change theory and is based on the argument that change is meaningful only if it deals with important issues. It is also critical that the initial change efforts result in actual changes in order to produce a culture of success.

Most large organizations that have planned large change efforts have started working with top management, which is trained and asked to produce a philosophy or values statement that will encourage lower-level managers to install participative practices. Top management is also helped to change its own behavior. Xerox, for example, has started using more task forces at the top and has started holding problem-solving work sessions. It has cut down on briefing sessions that often were simply for show-and-tell. Meeting rooms have been changed to encourage informality and problem solving. Flip charts and signs with guides to good group process have been added. Ford has done many of the same things and managers now come to meetings dressed informally.

In some cases, top management has even gone so far as to specify particular participative practices (Scanlon Plans, in the case of Dana Corporation, quality circles at Westinghouse). It is hard to argue with the idea of starting at the top, particularly if this produces a vision that can be shared with the rest of the organization. A vision can be very empowering of others and can support change efforts at lower levels. If it can be done, the top is probably the best place, but it is not the only place, to start.

It is quite possible to start change efforts at lower levels and to work upward. This approach has occurred at TRW and DEC, for example. It is generally slower than a top-down approach but it is the only way to start if top management is not ready to commit to organization-wide change. It also produces a high level of local commitment to what is done. At TRW, for example, the managers who have started new-design plants and gainsharing plans are strongly committed to these approaches because they have picked the approach that they feel is best for their situation.

Perhaps the best way of summarizing what has been said so far is that there are several places to start a change effort. The right place is where there is a desire to change; it is not necessarily at the top or the bottom. In this respect, to debate about bottom-up versus top-down change is too simplistic and unrealistic. On the other hand, in my experience, it is dangerous to initiate a change at the bottom without a strategy for dealing with the top. Perhaps the ideal situation starts with change at the top and finds that the rest of the organization is ready to change and has just been waiting for leadership.

No Right Program

The participative programs discussed so far are all possible candidates for starting a move toward high-involvement management; which one is best depends primarily on the present state of the organization. Choosing the right program can be critical in determining the success of the change effort. The further away from high-involvement management the organization is when it starts, the harder it will be to successfully adopt programs such as gainsharing and new-design plants. These programs change more things and, as a result, meet more resistance. Sometimes the resistance to change causes the entire participative approach to be rejected. If the programs work, however, they can move the organization forward at a much more rapid pace than is otherwise possible.

Thus, an organization should consider how much it has already pushed power, information, knowledge, and rewards downward. If it has done little of this, it may begin by utilizing such basic approaches as quality circles and survey feedback. Structured correctly, these can help an organization move toward a higher level of employee involvement.

If a low-level participative program is chosen, it is critical that the initial changes be followed by and supported by further changes that are congruent with participative management. Systems tend toward congruence, thus there is a good chance that a participative practice will be rejected unless other features of the organization are changed to support it. Thus, parallel structure efforts, such as quality circles and survey feedback, need to anticipate that they must rapidly move on to deal with how work is done in the core or regular organization. Similarly, single-feature change efforts, such as job enrichment, need to move quickly to deal with other aspects of the organization (unless, of course, they simply need to change one feature to be congruent with the rest of the system).

There are two exceptions to the general rule that any participative technique can start a change program. The first has to do with organized work settings. In these settings, there is usually no choice but to start with the QWL approach. This is the only effective approach to changing union-management relations. Thus, it should be used. It can change over time to be more participative but, in most cases, it is the only way to start.

The second has to do with new situations. Sometimes even very traditional organizations can start a new-design plant successfully. General Motors, General Foods, Scott Paper, and Procter & Gamble all have done this. Of course, this approach is not conflict-free—witness the case of the General Foods Topeka plant in which local management clashed with the rest of the organization. In the case of Procter & Gamble, virtually the entire manufacturing organization has been changed as a result of starting new-design plants. Procter & Gamble has become a high-involvement manufacturing organization because for over fifteen years all new plants have used the new-design approach. This leads to my next observation.

Resurrection Is More Difficult than Creation

The success rate in new plants is very high. In many cases, high-involvement systems have been installed quickly and the plants have operated at far-above-average performance levels. Recently, new organizations, such as People Express Airline, have started up in a highly participative mode. Thus, it appears that successful start-up of participative organizations is not limited to just new plants; it can extend to new organizations, as well.

The success rate of change efforts in existing organizations is much lower than the rate in new settings. Regardless of whether it is gainsharing, job redesign, QWL, or any other approach, a success rate of less than 75 percent is typical. In most pre-existing organizations, implementation of a complete high-involvement system has not occurred, even though the organization may have been successful in its adoption of a particular participative program.

If we acknowledge that creating new participative organizations is easier than changing old ones, we need to ask why. New organizations simply have a number of advantages when it comes to installing participative systems. A few of the most important advantages are: they can start with a congruent total system, they can select people who are compatible, no one has a vested interest in the status quo, and it is possible to deal with the whole organization at once so the participative island disease (to be discussed next) is avoided.

Given these advantages, it is hardly surprising that new situations have a much higher success rate. Indeed, even when we learn a lot more about how to change existing organizations, it is unlikely that it will ever be as easy or quick to change them as it is to establish new high-involvement ones. General Motors seems to have recognized this with their decision to invest billions of dollars in starting a new "company" to make the Saturn car. An existing plant could probably have been found, but it would have had a number of negative conditions that are not present in a new organization (such as resistance to change, traditional union contract, low trust, and vested interests). Thus, although General Motors' decision to start a new company may be seen as a waste of money, in fact it may be the only way that it can be competitive in the small-car business. Being successful today requires very different behavior from that which made General Motors successful in the past. The question that probably should be asked of General Motors is why it took so long to start changing, not why they are investing so much to create a new organization.

Participative Islands Often End Up Under Water

Frequently, organizations begin change projects by starting with small experimental groups. The reasons usually given
for this approach are: it provides a chance for the organization
to learn, it can test out the approach to see if it works, and it
does not require a large amount of resources to start. There are
two major problems with this approach, however. First, having
an experimental group is of limited value both as a learning experience and as a test because it is qualitatively and quantita-
tively different from having a high-involvement organization.
Second, experimental groups rarely survive for very long when
standing by themselves in the middle of a hostile environment.
Let us look at these two points in more detail.

Having a single participative group is clearly quantitative-
ly different from having all groups operating in this mode. What
is less obvious and more interesting is the fact that it is often
also qualitatively different because the surrounding circumstances are radically different when a group is embedded in a
participative situation. Organizational policies and practices are
more likely to be supportive and education from others is more
readily available. This results in a greater likelihood of success
for participative work areas that are imbedded in participative
systems. In addition, managing them is different because the
key issues are less ones of protecting the groups against hostile
forces and more ones of helping the group develop. Finally,
groups that start as "experiments" often see themselves and are
seen as temporary. As a result, they may not put forth the effort that is required for success. On the other hand, when the
decision is made that this is the way it is going to be, ways to
make it work tend to be found because there is no going back.

Little research has been done on institutionalizing experimental groups, but there is some evidence that it often fails to
happen. This is hardly surprising given what has been said so far
about the importance of total-system congruence and the social
psychology finding that deviants are rejected and pressured to
conform. Unless the experimental areas are clearly separated

from the rest of the organization, there is every reason to believe that overwhelming pressures will build up toward congruence.

This discussion should not be construed to mean that an organization should not use the experimental-group idea in a change effort. It does suggest, however, that it should be used cautiously and with full knowledge of its limitations. In general, it should probably only be used when the organization is willing to establish several groups that are not experimental, but merely the first areas to be changed as part of a total-system-change effort. Only if this is done are the groups likely to be successful enough and to survive long enough for other groups to be formed.

It Is Hard to Kill a Good Thing

So far our discussion has focused on changing in the direction of high-involvement management. There is, however, a second kind of change effort that is of considerable theoretical and practical interest. It is an effort directed toward changing high-involvement systems to more traditional ones. At first glance, it might seem that this would be very easy to do because often democratic systems have proven easy victims for autocratic leaders and, as noted, "participative islands" often end up under water. Nevertheless, there is evidence that under certain conditions, it can be quite difficult to dislodge participative systems once they have become fully established. In fact, it may be as hard, or harder, to dislodge them as it is to dislodge top-down traditional management.

People become comfortable with participative practices and can be expected to resist any change. In addition, any change effort that deals only with a limited number of factors is likely to fail because the weight of the case will be on the side of high-involvement management and the systems will tend to seek congruence. In this case, congruence will mean reversing the movement away from participative management.

Essential to the argument that high-involvement organizations are difficult to change is the view that even lower-level participants in work organizations have power and their desires can make a difference. They have power in a number of respects, including the ability to unionize, strike, quit, slow down production, and file court cases. It is precisely because they have power that the destruction of an attractive approach to management is difficult.

There is some evidence on just how difficult it is to change participative work systems. One widely reported "successful" change case is the General Foods Topeka plant. (Incidentally, this plant was recently sold by General Foods, perhaps because it finally got tired of dealing with all the issues it raised for them.) According to reports, after great initial success as a participative plant this new plant was changed to a more traditional approach to management. These reports make good reading but, to the best of my knowledge, they are wrong. It is true that the key managers were replaced with the objective of making the plant more like (read as less participative than) other General Food plants. Several traditional managers were installed, but, according to my reports, the participative system still operates effectively because the employees were successful in resisting most changes to it.

The experience at Topeka is similar to those at two other plants of which I am aware. In both cases, "traditional" plant managers were put in charge of participative plants. The result in both cases was the same—the system survived and the new managers became strong supporters of them.

Unions can play a potentially decisive role in assuring that participative systems survive. When they share responsibility for the creation of a participative system it is hard to imagine their allowing management to change to a traditional system. For example, in the case of Saturn, the UAW can hardly allow General Motors to revert to traditional management.

Overall, there is not enough evidence to irrevocably establish that participative approaches are difficult to eliminate, but there are a number of reasons why they may be quite difficult to eliminate once they are established.

Vision Is Critical

One characteristic that frequently separates successful change projects from unsuccessful ones is the existence of a vision. Walt Disney is often quoted as saying if you can dream it, you can do it. In the case of organizational change, a slightly different expression is appropriate: dreaming it is the beginning of it. In the successful projects I have studied, there is usually a shared vision about what the desired end state is. The issues of management and control have been successfully reframed into a participative way of thinking. In unsuccessful projects, the participants rarely have a clear idea of where they would like to take the organization, and they lack a clear overview of how all the pieces fit together. In short, they tend to see the trees, not the forest.

When individuals have a good overview or vision, they develop heuristics or decision rules that allow them to make good decisions about the details of implementing particular changes. This allows them to reject or accept specific policies and practices and to deal with people in a consistent way. When they lack a vision or overall philosophy of what they are trying to accomplish, then each decision cannot be tested against overarching principles. The result is that decisions tend to be haphazard and a lack of consistency and congruence is apparent in the change effort. This results in poorly designed changes and often a tendency for the system to bog down in details and minutiae.

Exhibit 2 provides an example of the "vision" created by Honeywell. It is Honeywell's attempt to say what it wants to stand for as an organization and how it wants to manage and deal with people. Exhibit 3 provides another example, this one from a newly independent telephone company, Pacific Telesis.

A key reason why the language and symbols used by People Express Airline work is that they are supported by a vision of what an involvement-oriented airline should be. This vision includes making every employee a self-managing owner who understands and cares about the business. In order to be success-

Exhibit 2. Honeywell Principles.

Honeywell is an international corporation whose goal is to work together with customers to develop and apply advanced technologies through products, systems, and services, which in turn serve primarily to improve productivity, conserve resources, and meet aerospace and defense needs. Honeywell adheres to the following principles.

- *Profits.* Profitable operations are necessary to assure the continued health and growth of the company. Honeywell expects profits which equal or exceed those of leading international companies.
- *Integrity.* Honeywell believes in the highest level of integrity and ethical behavior in relationships with customers, employees, shareholders, vendors, neighbors, and governments.
- *Customers.* Honeywell is dedicated to serving customers through excellence of product, systems, and service, and through working together with customers to find the answers to their problems.
- *People.* People are key to Honeywell's success. The company actively and affirmatively attracts and promotes the best people without regard to age, race, sex, creed, disability, or nationality, and rewards them on their performance. Honeywell provides an environment for open, timely communications, safe working conditions, and opportunities for personal growth and accomplishment. Honeywell respects the dignity and privacy of individuals and believes in a climate of trust, cooperation and employee involvement.
- *Quality.* Quality of product, application, and service is essential to continue Honeywell's success. Quality improvement should pervade every job within the company. Honeywell believes quality results from an environment in which people work together to sustain excellence.
- *Decision making.* Honeywell believes sound growth is necessary to successful company performance. This is achieved through well-managed risk taking, innovation, and entrepreneurship. Honeywell is committed to a decentralized structure in which business decisions are made at the lowest appropriate level.
- *Citizenship.* Honeywell operates in compliance with all applicable laws and in ways that build a lasting reputation for integrity and good citizenship in all countries where it does business. The company encourages employees to become involved in community and national affairs. Honeywell manages its business in ways that are sensitive to the environment and that conserve natural resources.

Source: An internal publication of Honeywell Corporation.

ful, organizational change projects need to instill a collective vision of what the desired end state should be. This is easier said than done. It is not a simple matter to develop such a shared vision.

Exhibit 3. Pacific Telesis Commitments.

- *We are customer focused.* We have a personal and uncompromising focus on the individual customer. We keep our commitments and are reliable and easy to do business with. We measure customer satisfaction to promote this focus. We emphasize teamwork and simplicity of process to achieve competitive performance in the marketplace.
- *We deliver on the bottom line.* We embrace the importance of profits and earnings growth which best serve the long-term interests of our investors, customers, and employees. We staff, organize, and measure our business to support this focus. We make current decisions in light of long-term interests.
- *We are creative, can-do people.* We have the freedom to act and innovate to meet our customer's needs as though each of us owned the business. Strategy guides our direction; sound judgment guides our daily execution. We take prudent risks and are each accountable for our actions.
- *We value the individual.* We believe in personal responsibility, initiative, and participation, so that everyone has a stake in the business. We reward contributions, knowing that success depends on people. We provide our people with continuing career-development opportunities, in the interest of individual growth opportunities and to build sound business leadership capability.
- *We communicate to get the job done.* We keep each other informed. We clearly communicate our expectations and our progress toward achieving them in a continuous, ongoing manner. We encourage informal, candid communication among whomever needs to talk. We believe in leadership and involvement to get the job done.
- *We are the best at what we do.* We are committed to quality in everything we do and to technological leadership. We "do it right the first time." We obtain, retain, and develop the best people available, believing nothing is more critical to our long-term success. We have high expectations for ourselves as we pursue excellence and quality in every aspect of our business endeavors.

Source: An internal publication of Pacific Telesis.

I have tried a number of approaches to building shared visions. These include reading articles and books, visiting other organizations, long discussions with key management groups, and exercises designed to help the people identify their ideal model. For example, I have often taken managers to visit high-involvement plants. In many cases, talking to production employees who understand the business has been essential in helping managers realize what a high-involvement organization can be. Many things can help people develop a vision, but in my experience, it

is difficult to move some people in this direction. It requires
thinking at a rather abstract level and some people simply find
this very difficult to do.

In short, you can help somebody develop a concept of
what they are trying to do with an organization, but certain in-
clinations and natural abilities are needed. It is impossible to
guarantee that an organization will be able to develop the kind
of conceptual model that is needed. Also, in many successful
change projects, these skills and partially developed conceptual
models were present in people's heads before a consultant ever
entered the scene. All the consultant did was to help develop
the existing framework.

As was noted earlier, it is often best to have top management create the vision first. This has been done at Motorola,
Honeywell, and People Express. If this is not possible, as was the
case in DEC and TRW, others in the organization can sometimes create it and get it widely adopted by the organization.
Indeed, this bubble-up process has a great deal to recommend it
(Cleveland, 1985), since it is congruent with the values of participative management.

Values Can Energize Change Programs

The scientific literature on organizational change often
presents the process as a rather antiseptic one in which a new
method and its possible outcomes are described to an organization and the organization then decides whether to adopt or
reject it. Energy for the change is assumed to come from the
presumed advantages of the change. Often the values of the participants and their impact on the change process are ignored.

Major changes require the commitment of tremendous
time and energy. Therefore, the energy issue is critical. In my
experience, it is difficult to mobilize the needed energy on the
basis of a purely rational analysis of the advantages and disadvantages. This is where values and beliefs come into play.

In some change efforts, successful appeals to the employee's values have been used to provide energy for the change.
The change agent or other leaders of the change program
talk about the underlying values that guide the project. For

example, in the change project at Harmon Industries in Bolivar, Tennessee, Michael Maccoby talked about such values as democracy, equity, and individualization. He successfully used these to support the specific changes that were implemented (Macy, 1979). In many respects, this proved to be a very effective strategy because the values stated were strongly held by the participants, who wished to see them promoted.

This example implies that organizational change can be stimulated by appealing to employee values, especially when changing toward high-involvement management. Openness, participative decision making, personal growth and development, and financial sharing are basic American values. They are not the wild ideas of a group of academics or liberals, but are values that most people already accept and that portions of society try to operate by right now.

Political scientists and others who are interested in social reform and revolution have known about the importance of values for a long time. Apparently, organizations are no different—change can be aided by a skillful appeal to values, especially when they relate to the service or product an organization produces. Organizations that do socially important things can appeal to people in ways that organizations who are "just" in business to make a buck cannot. For example, a junk-food manufacturer simply cannot claim the same high sense of social purpose that a hospital or public service organization can.

My Data Are Not Their Data

Most writings on how to conduct organizational change projects stress the importance of evaluating the success of the change effort. They talk about the financial, attitudinal, and behavioral data that can be collected to support evaluation of the project. In many of the change projects I have been involved with, an effort has been made to gather this kind of "objective" data (Lawler, Nadler, and Cammann, 1980). One problem has consistently developed, however. The people in the organization tend not to use these "scientific" data when they evaluate the success or failure of the effort.

They often express interest in the data, but, for a number

of reasons, evaluate the project based on other factors. In many cases, the evaluations are based on odd pieces of circumstantial data or happenstance. For example, at one location a top-level manager walked into the plant and casually asked a worker how he liked the project. The worker said that not much was happening. The executive turned to me and said "see, I told you it wouldn't work," and from then on he was very resistant to any data that suggested that the project was going well. In another case, the reverse happened. The key decision maker encountered several workers who raved about the project. From then on, he was strongly committed to the project, despite the fact that the economic data showed no financial effect of the project. Ironically, the same individual had stressed at the beginning of the project that he would be convinced only if we could show strong financial change as a result of the project.

What seems to be happening in these two cases and in many others is that people in decision-making positions tend to make ongoing real-time evaluations of change efforts. Since they are unschooled in data and data collection, they are often strongly influenced in these evaluations by haphazardly collected and often misleading data. In summary, the researcher's data are not their data and, often by the time we get around to doing a thorough evaluation of a project, it has been either written off as a failure or declared a large success in the organization.

Declaring a Success Can Contribute to Success

I have studied several projects that developed a very high profile (for example, the Bolivar UAW/Harmon Industries project). The participants in these projects frequently appeared in magazines, newspapers, and on television and radio shows. Surprisingly, these appearances came very early in the history of the projects. In many cases, they came so early in the projects that little evidence was available to indicate whether the project was successful or not. This, however, did not stop the sponsors of the projects from declaring publicly that the projects were successful. Participants in the projects seemed to fall into a similar mode when they appeared in public. In essence, they declared the projects a success and talked about their wonders before significant outcomes had been produced.

What was the effect of these premature declarations of success? To a degree, they seemed to energize the participants to make the projects successful because they had become publicly committed to the fact that the projects were successful. Of course, this public declaration of success did not prevent them from talking privately about the limitations and the shortcomings of their change projects. This was still a heated topic of discussion. Nevertheless, it seemed that the premature declarations of success were more helpful than harmful since many of the projects did later enjoy some substantial success.

Planned Change Efforts Rarely Go as Planned

In most change efforts rather detailed plans concerning the nature of the changes are developed before action starts. In most cases, however, within a year, the original plan has to be abandoned, and in some cases, the change effort has taken on a different approach to installing high-involvement management. For example, the Bolivar project, a program that began with a plan to get people more involved in their work through creating self-managing work groups, ended up giving them the chance to go home early when they increased their productivity. In another case, an experiment in introducing a gainsharing plan in one part of a company ended up changing the base pay of everyone in the company. What these and many other examples suggest is that it is difficult to plan change, particularly when the implementation process has a built-in high degree of participation. The only thing that can actually be planned is the process of change.

A crucial part of the change process should be the adoption of a learning stance. Organizations need to try things, see how they work, learn from this, and improve them. It is unreasonable to expect to "get it right" the first time. There are simply too many conditions to consider to expect success on the first try. Furthermore, situations change so that what might have been right becomes wrong. The only way to deal with it is to regularly change the program. For example, the successful gainsharing plans at both Herman Miller and Donnelly Mirrors have changed many times over their more than thirty years. Their basic philosophies have not changed but their operating details have, thus reflecting changes in the business as well as in society. It is to the credit of these organizations that they have made these changes and have continually evaluated their participative-management programs.

For the implementer of change, this suggests that the adoption of an adaptive/opportunistic stance is crucial. If the implementers rigidly maintain an insistence on sticking to the "original plan," they may find themselves expendable because they are standing in the way of progress. The point, of course, is that the movement toward high-involvement management requires leadership, but that rigid autocratic leaders will have trouble retaining their positions. Organizations do not lend themselves to rigidly imposed change programs. One reason for this is that they are constantly being buffeted by a changing environment that demands adaptation for survival. Thus, a plan that looks good at the beginning of a change program may not look good later in the implementation process.

In addition, organizations are made up of individuals with different values, preferences, and power positions. It is almost impossible to take all of these into account in designing a change program, even if there is widespread participation in the design activities. However, once a change starts unfolding, many of these must be taken into account and the change must be altered and adapted. The program must also be flexible enough to take advantage of opportunities when they present themselves. For example, the building of a new plant, a quality problem, and the growth in demand for a product can all present unexpected opportunities for moving toward high-involvement management.

Overall, planned change is not impossible, but it is often difficult. The key point here is that change is an ongoing process, and it is incorrect to think that a visionary end state can be reached in a highly programmed way. When a change toward high-involvement management is the objective, it may be best to speak of guided change rather than planned change.

Think Long-Term

One of the most common mistakes in change efforts is to expect quick results. Some participative programs can, in fact, produce some positive results in a matter of months, but organization-wide change efforts typically cannot. Gainsharing plans and quality-circle programs, for example, can often produce relatively quick improvements in productivity and quality. Other programs, such as QWL projects, take much longer (often several years) to produce results.

Organization-wide change in a large organization is an entirely different matter: it can take decades. For example, General Motors started moving toward participative management during the 1960s, with several projects in plants. Decades later, it has not changed all plants nor has it achieved high-involvement management in any location. If things go as planned, the Saturn Company may be its first! Admittedly, General Motors started close to ground zero as far as participative management is concerned; in addition, it is a very large organization and has committed only limited resources to participative management. Nevertheless, its slow pace of change is instructive. I told Ford when it began its program to consider a decade of change. The change programs at Motorola and Weyerhaeuser have already lasted about a decade and, although they show positive results, they certainly are not finished.

Overall, moving to participative management is a long, slow, somewhat chaotic process. It means following an unclear map and regularly adapting to external change and internal learning. Is it worth it? It is, if it represents the only viable way to operate.

References

Argyris, C. *Personality and Organization.* New York: Harper & Row, 1957.

Bennis, W., and Nanus, B. *Leaders.* New York: Harper & Row, 1985.

Bowers, D. G. "OD Techniques and Their Results in 23 Organizations: The Michigan ICL Study." *Journal of Applied Behavior Science,* 1973, *9,* 21-43.

Bowers, D. G., and Franklin, J. L. "Survey-Guided Development: Using Human Resources Measurement in Organizational Change." *Journal of Contemporary Business,* 1972, *1,* 43-55.

Bullock, R. J., and Bullock, P. F. "Gainsharing and Rubik's Cube: Solving System Problems." *National Productivity Review,* 1982, *2* (1), 396-407.

Bullock, R. J., and Lawler, E. E. "Gainsharing: A Few Questions, and Fewer Answers." *Human Resource Management,* 1984, *23* (1), 23-40.

Burns, J. M. *Leadership.* New York: Harper & Row, 1978.

Cleveland, H. "Control: The Twilight of Hierarchy." *New Management,* 1985, *3* (2), 14-25.

Coch, L., and French, J. R. P. "Overcoming Resistance to Change." *Human Relations,* 1949, *1* (4), 512-533.

Cohen-Rosenthal, E. "Orienting Labor-Management Coopera-tion Toward Revenue and Growth." *National Productivity Review,* 1985, *4* (4), 385–396.

Cole, R. E. "Made in Japan—Quality Control Circles." *Across the Board,* 1979, *16* (11), 72–78.

Cole, R. E. "Target Information for Competitive Performance." *Harvard Business Review,* 1985, *63* (3), 100–109.

Cole, R. E., and Tachiki, D. S. "Forging International Links: Making Quality Circles Work in the U.S." *National Productiv-ity Review,* 1984, *3* (4), 407–429.

Copenhaver, L., and Guest, R. H. "Quality of Work Life: The Anatomy of Two Successes." *National Productivity Review,* 1982, *1* (4), 5–12.

Crosby, P. B. *Quality Is Free.* New York: McGraw-Hill, 1979.

Cummings, T. G. "Self-Regulating Workgroups: A Socio-Techni-cal Synthesis." *Academy of Management Review,* 1978, *3,* 625–633.

Cummings, T. G., and Molloy, E. S. *Improving Productivity and the Quality of Work Life.* New York: Praeger, 1977.

Dulworth, M. *Employee Involvement and Gainsharing Produce Dramatic Results at Eggers Industries.* Washington, D.C.: U.S. Department of Labor, 1985.

Ewing, D. W. *Freedom Inside the Organization.* New York: Dut-ton, 1977.

Ewing, D. W. *Do It My Way Or You're Fired.* New York: Wiley, 1983.

Flamholtz, E. G. *Human Resource Accounting.* Encino, Calif.: Dickenson, 1974.

Ford, R. N. *Motivation Through the Work Itself.* New York: American Management Association, 1969.

Fortune Magazine Editors. *Working Smarter.* New York: Viking, 1982.

Goodman, P. *Assessing Organizational Change: The Rushton Quality of Work Experiment.* New York: Wiley Interscience, 1979.

Gorlin, H., and Schein, L. *Innovations in Managing Human Re-sources.* New York: Conference Board, 1984.

Guest, R. H. "Quality of Worklife—Learning From Tarrytown." *Harvard Business Review,* 1979, *57* (4), 76–87.

Hackman, J. R., and Lawler, E. E. "Employee Reactions to Job Characteristics." *Journal of Applied Psychology,* 1971, *55,* 259-286.

Hackman, J. R., and Oldham, G. R. *Work Redesign.* Reading, Mass.: Addison-Wesley, 1980.

Hanlon, M. D., Nadler, D. A., and Gladstein, D. *Attempting Work Reform.* New York: Wiley Interscience, 1985.

Herzberg, F. *Work and the Nature of Man.* Cleveland, Ohio: World, 1966.

Kanarick, A. F., and Dotlich, D. L. "Honeywell's Agenda for Organizational Change." *New Management,* 1984, *2* (1), 14-19.

Kerr, C., and Rosow, J. M. (eds.). *Work in America: The Decade Ahead.* New York: D. Van Nostrand, 1979.

Kilmann, R. H. *Beyond the Quick Fix: Managing Five Tracks to Organizational Success.* San Francisco: Jossey-Bass, 1984.

Kopelman, R. E. "Job Redesign and Productivity: A Review of the Evidence." *National Productivity Review,* 1985, *4* (3), 237-255.

Lawler, E. E. "Job Design and Employee Motivation." *Personnel Psychology,* 1969, *22,* 426-435.

Lawler, E. E. *Pay and Organizational Effectiveness: A Psychological View.* New York: McGraw-Hill, 1971.

Lawler, E. E. *Motivation in Work Organizations.* Monterey, Calif.: Brooks/Cole, 1973.

Lawler, E. E. "The New Plant Revolution." *Organizational Dynamics,* 1978, *6* (3), 2-12.

Lawler, E. E. *Pay and Organization Development.* Reading, Mass.: Addison-Wesley, 1981.

Lawler, E. E. "Education, Management Style, and Organizational Effectiveness." *Personnel Psychology,* 1985, *38* (1), 1-26.

Lawler, E. E., and Ledford, G. E. "Productivity and the Quality of Worklife." *National Productivity Review,* 1982, *1,* 23-36.

Lawler, E. E., and Ledford, G. E. "Skill Based Pay." *Personnel,* 1985, *62* (9), 30-37.

Lawler, E. E., and Mohrman, S. A. "Quality Circles After the Fad." *Harvard Business Review,* 1985, *85* (1), 64-71.

Lawler, E. E., Nadler, D. A., and Cammann, C. *Organizational Assessment.* New York: Wiley, 1980.

Lawler, E. E., and Ozley, L. "Winning Union-Management Corporation on Quality of Work Life Projects." *Management Review,* 1979, *68* (3), 1924.

Lawler, E. E., Renwick, P. A., and Bullock, R. J. "Employee Influence on Decisions: An Analysis." *Journal of Occupational Behavior,* 1981, *2,* 115–123.

Lawler, E. E., and Rhode, J. G. *Information and Control in Organizations.* Pacific Palisades, Calif.: Goodyear, 1976.

Lesieur, F. G. (ed.). *The Scanlon Plan.* Cambridge, Mass.: MIT Press, 1958.

Lesieur, F. G., and Puckett, E. S. "The Scanlon Plan Has Proved Itself." *Harvard Business Review,* 1969, *47* (5), 109–118.

Likert, R. *New Patterns of Management.* New York: McGraw-Hill, 1961.

Locke, E. A., and Latham, G. P. *Goal Setting: A Motivational Technique that Works.* Englewood Cliffs, N.J.: Prentice-Hall, 1984.

Locke, E. A., and others. "The Relative Effectiveness of Four Methods of Motivating Employee Performance." In K. D. Duncan, M. M. Greeneberg, and D. Wallis (eds.), *Changes in Working Life.* Chichester, England: Wiley, 1980.

McGregor, D. *The Human Side of Enterprise.* New York: McGraw-Hill, 1960.

Macy, B. A. "Progress Report on the Bolivar Quality of Work Experiment." *Personnel Journal,* 1979, *20* (8), 527–559.

Maslow, A. H. *Motivation and Personality.* New York: Harper & Row, 1954.

Metzger, B. L. *Profit Sharing in 38 Large Companies.* Evanston, Ill.: Profit Sharing Research Foundation, 1975.

Mirvis, P. H., and Lawler, E. E. "Accounting for the Quality of Work Life." *Journal of Occupational Behavior,* 1984, *5,* 197–212.

Mohrman, A. M., and Lawler, E. E. "The Diffusion of QWL as a Paradigm Shift." In W. G. Bennis, K. D. Benne, and R. Chin (eds.), *The Planning of Change.* New York: Holt, Rinehart & Winston, 1985.

Moore, B. E., and Ross, T. L. *The Scanlon Way to Improved Productivity.* New York: Wiley, 1978.

Nadler, D. A. *Feedback and Organizational Development.* Reading, Mass.: Addison-Wesley, 1977.

Nadler, D. A., Hanlon, M., and Lawler, E. E. "Factors Influencing the Success of Labor-Management Quality of Work Life Projects." *Journal of Occupational Behavior,* 1980, *1,* 53–67.

Naisbitt, J. *Megatrends.* New York: Warner, 1982.

Naisbitt, J., and Aburdene, P. *Reinventing the Corporate Future.* New York: Warner, 1985.

New York Stock Exchange. *People and Productivity.* New York: New York Stock Exchange, 1982.

Nurick, A. J. *Participation in Organization Change.* New York: Praeger, 1985.

Nystrom, P. C., and Starbuck, W. H. *Handbook of Organizational Design.* Oxford, England: Oxford University Press, 1981.

O'Boyle, T. F. "Loyalty Ebbs at Many Companies as Employees Grow Disillusioned." *Wall Street Journal,* July 11, 1985, p. 29.

O'Toole, J. *Work, Learning, and the American Future.* San Francisco: Jossey-Bass, 1977.

O'Toole, J. *Making America Work.* New York: Continuum, 1981.

O'Toole, J. *Vanguard Management.* New York: Doubleday, 1985.

Ouchi, W. *Theory Z.* Reading, Mass.: Addison-Wesley, 1981.

Pascarella, P. "Quality Circles." *Industry Week,* 1982, *213* (7), 50–55.

Perkins, D., Nieva, V., and Lawler, E. *Managing Creation: The Challenge of Building a New Organization.* New York: Wiley, 1983.

Perry, B. *Enfield: A High Performance System.* Bedford, Mass.: Educational Services Development and Publishing, 1984.

Peters, T. J., and Austin, N. *A Passion for Excellence.* New York: Random House, 1985.

Peters, T. J., and Waterman, R. H. *In Search of Excellence: Lessons from America's Best Run Companies.* New York: Harper & Row, 1982.

Pinder, C. *Work Motivation*. Glenview, Ill.: Scott, Foresman, 1984.

Reich, R. E. "The Executive's New Clothes." *New Republic*, May 1985, pp. 23-28.

Rosow, J. (ed.). *Productivity Prospects for Growth*. New York: D. Van Nostrand, 1981.

Rosow, J. *Employment Security in a Free Economy*. New York: Pergamon Press, 1984.

Schlesinger, L. A. *Quality of Work Life and the Supervisor*. New York: Praeger, 1982.

Seashore, S. E. "Quality of Working Life Perspective." In A. Van de Ven and W. F. Joyce (eds.), *Perspectives on Organization Design and Behavior*. New York: Wiley Interscience, 1981.

Seashore, S. E., and Bowers, D. G. "The Durability of Organizational Change." *American Psychologist*, 1970, *25* (3), 227-233.

Seashore, S., Lawler, E., Mirvis, P., and Cammann, C. *Observing and Measuring Organizational Change: A Guide to Field Practice*. New York: Wiley, 1983.

Servan-Schreiber, J. J. *The American Challenge*. New York: Atheneum, 1968.

Simmons, J., and Mares, W. *Working Together*. New York: Knopf, 1983.

Tannenbaum, R., and Schmidt, W. "How to Choose a Leadership Pattern." *Harvard Business Review*, 1958, *36*, 95-101.

Taylor, F. W. *The Principles of Scientific Management*. New York: Harper & Row, 1911.

Taylor, J. C., and Bowers, D. G. *Survey of Organizations: A Machine Scored Standardized Questionnaire Instrument*. Ann Arbor, Mich.: Institute for Social Research, 1972.

Trist, E. L., and Bamforth, K. W. "Some Social Psychological Consequences of the Longwall Method of Coal-Getting." *Human Relations*, 1951, *4*, 3-38.

Vroom, V. H. *Work and Motivation*. New York: Wiley, 1964.

Vroom, V. H., and Yetton, P. W. *Leadership and Decision-Making*. Pittsburgh, Pa.: University of Pittsburgh Press, 1973.

Walker, C. R., and Guest, R. H. *The Man on the Assembly Line*. Cambridge, Mass.: Harvard University Press, 1952.

Walton, R. E. "From Control to Commitment in the Work-place." *Harvard Business Review,* 1985, *63* (2), 76–84.

Walton, R. E., and McKersie, R. B. *A Behavioral Theory of Labor Negotiations.* New York: McGraw-Hill, 1965.

Walton, R. E., and Schlesinger, L. A. "Do Supervisors Thrive in Participative Work Systems?" *Organizational Dynamics,* 1979, *8* (3), 24–39.

Work in America. Cambridge, Mass.: MIT Press, 1973.

Yankelovich, D. *Putting the Work Ethic to Work.* New York: Public Agenda Foundation, 1983.

Zaleznik, A. "Managers and Leaders: Are They Different?" *Harvard Business Review,* 1977, *55* (3), 67–78.

Index